THEY WERE BLACK. ALL BLACK.

A HIGH SCHOOL SUCCESS STORY

DARYL ROCK

Rock Academic Services LLC
Brooklyn, New York

They Were Black. All Black.
A High School Success Story

Names: Rock, Daryl, author.
Title: They were Black. All Black: a high school success story / by Daryl Rock.
Description: First edition. | [Brooklyn, New York]: [Rock Academic Services LLC], [2026]
Identifiers: LCCN: 2025950230 | ISBN: 9798999364906 (Paperback) | 9798999364926 (Hardcover) | 9798999364913 (Digital)
Subjects: LCSH: Benjamin Banneker Academy for Community Development (Brooklyn, NY) | Benjamin Banneker Academy for Community Development (Brooklyn, NY)--Basketball. | Education, Urban--New York (State)--New York. | Urban schools--New York (State)--New York. | High school students, Black--New York (State)--New York. | Educational equalization--New York (State)--New York. | Brooklyn (New York, N.Y.)--Social life and customs. | Anti-racism--United States. | Social justice--United States. | Achievement motivation in youth--New York (State)--New York. | Academic achievement--New York (State)--New York. | Teacher-student relationships--New York (State)--New York. | Racism in education--United States. | Multicultural education--New York (State)--New York. | Teachers--Training of--United States. | Educational change--United States. | Education and state--United States. | Educational accountability--United States. | Critical race theory--United States. | School management and organization--United States. | Segregation in education--United States. | Black people--Segregation--United States. | BISAC: EDUCATION / Multicultural Education. | EDUCATION / Urban. | EDUCATION / Cultural Pedagogies.
Classification: LCC: LC5133.N5 R63 2026 | DDC: 379.1/0974723--dc23

Front cover image by the artist.
Book design by Leon Ogellac.

For all the Black Warrior educators whose
strength and courage shaped the path and whose
work still lights the way.

TABLE OF CONTENTS

INTRODUCTION

Benjamin Banneker Academy for Community Development, also known as Banneker, is a high school in Brooklyn, New York, established in 1993 by New York politician Roger Green and several other community leaders.

The school building, a former Drake's Cake factory, was in the pre-gentrified neighborhood of Clinton Hill, Brooklyn, at the time of its opening. I was the school's principal for ten years. Before arriving at Banneker, I taught math at the middle, high school, and college levels. While working as an educator, I acquired two master's degrees and a doctorate in education from New York University. The year I left Banneker, we had the highest graduation rate for Black students in New York State (97 percent).[1] The school had 96 percent Black and Latino students, with a 92 percent Black and Latino teacher staff.

I decided to write *They Were Black. All Black: A High School Success Story* to share my experience during those incredible years working with so many talented students, gifted teachers, hands-on parents, and the community that supported us. We created a successful model that can be replicated across this country in any school where Black and Brown students struggle to learn and excel. The model for Banneker and its unequivocal success was based on the early segregated schools in the Southern United States, and I will share the similarities.

This book outlines and unpacks our process, culture, challenges, and accomplishments, with the final two chapters devoted to providing recommendations for schools and districts to improve outcomes. *They Were Black. All Black.* has a second storyline that chronicles the boys' basketball team's 2000–2001 season. At the beginning of each chapter, there is a short dialogue between the basketball coach and me in my office. We had these conversations regularly throughout the year. These exchanges give readers a sense of the ebb and flow of a Banneker basketball season alongside some of the school's day-to-day happenings.

I was a basketball coach myself, and I used the game as a vital tool to reach many young people. I believe the only relationship stronger than that of coach and athlete is that of parent and child. I love the game and promoted it wherever I worked. Many well-meaning educators view basketball as a distraction, but I see it differently. The game boosts self-esteem, teaches lifelong leadership skills, and is an art form. It promotes health, gets kids moving, helps players follow established rules, and teaches them how to get along with others. Besides the dialogue with the coach, there will be other references to the game of basketball as it pertains to Black culture.

Readers will also find direct quotes from actual Banneker students and teachers describing their personal experiences at the school. These quotes are placed throughout the book, offering first-hand, unedited accounts of the school and the atmosphere we intentionally created.

It will quickly become apparent that the heroes of this narrative are Black and Brown educators. This high school success story is deeply rooted in unapologetic love and respect for Black life and the Black experience. White educators are not at the center of the Banneker story, nor is this book about white teacher-bashing. I find that counterproductive. My goal for this book is to show readers what can happen when

THEY WERE BLACK. ALL BLACK.

Black students are educated by dedicated Black teachers who have established an environment that uplifts and celebrates Black legacy, contributions, and excellence. I hope that our achievements and efforts at Banneker will inspire readers to recognize what is possible, despite two significant challenges: 1) the current national narrative about failing schools and 2) the push to remove Black History from the curriculum. Black students can thrive, and the solutions are right in front of us. Welcome to this *Black Love Story*.

* * *

At Benjamin Banneker Academy, the principal's office on the first floor looks out on the high school's main lobby. Students and staff come in and out throughout the day. A large wooden desk is situated in the center of the room with two soft chairs facing inward, and an oversized couch is positioned in the background. On one wall, we see three medium-sized paintings of basketball players by artist Richard Barclift, and the adjacent wall has several black-and-white framed photos of early African American classrooms circa 1920.

Coach Wendell Saunders and I met regularly in my office throughout the year to discuss the progress of the basketball team. What follows is the first of several dialogues between us during the 2000–2001 season, offering insight into the school and the dynamics of the basketball program. This initial conversation sets the stage for the season ahead.

Principal's Office, Benjamin Banneker High School, Brooklyn, New York

September 6, 2000

Rock: How are things, Coach? You had a good summer?

Coach: Not bad, Rock. Looking forward to a good year.

Rock: How's the team looking? I saw Gary over the summer at Gershwin Park. He doesn't look like the same kid. He was killing them. He is about 6'5", playing against grown men and dominating for a fifteen-year-old going into his second year of high school. Last year, he looked like an awkward, skinny kid, but if he keeps playing like he does, he may get recruited by a D-1 college. How does the rest of the squad look? Is everyone back? Any talented new kids? Any strong prospects?

Coach: Guess you haven't heard, Rock.

Rock: Heard what?

Coach: Gary transferred out.

Rock: What? No way, Coach!

Coach: Yup! Gary transferred. He's not here anymore.

Rock: Damn! Where is he going?

Coach: Catholic High.

Rock: They took him. His mother is okay with that?

Coach: I guess so. He didn't say anything to me. Neither did his parents. I found out yesterday. Guess his parents thought it would be better for his career. Catholic High has a stronger basketball reputation than we do, and they have an excellent coach.

Rock: Damn, Coach, the day before school starts. What about the other guys?

Coach: Kareem is back and had a good summer. We may have a couple of kids who want to transfer in. Parents are starting to notice Banneker for its academics.

Rock: Talk to the guidance counselor. I think there are some openings in the junior and senior classes. Let me know when you have tryouts. *Damn, Gary left…*

1

WHY THIS STORY NOW

During my time at Banneker, I was given the support and opportunities needed to expand my possibilities in life. I was taught self-worth and pride in myself as a young Black girl from the "ghetto" with aspirations to become a doctor. I took this pride with me as I entered predominantly white institutions for college and medical school. I knew the history of my people and the beautiful struggle they fought for me to have opportunities. I am forever grateful to have been taught the history of our people and to discuss our future with such amazing teachers. —K. Woodroof, Class of 2001

Banneker was good for my soul! It taught me self-love and how to be around people who looked like me, and to be proud. It definitely shaped who I am today, and I still feel very fortunate to have been a student. —G. Hazelwood, Class of 2008

Before using the title, *They Were Black. All Black: A High School Success Story,* I originally planned to name this book *Sit Your Black Ass Down.* But I thought too many people would see this as a slur or a command to discipline

Black children. That title came to me while teaching graduate students at Hunter College in New York City. One evening before class, I noticed several white students, first-year elementary school teachers, milling around in the back of the classroom, having a heated discussion. When I asked what was going on, one of them said, "Something happened in my elementary classroom today that was unfair and upsetting." They all seemed embarrassed to tell me, but I coaxed it out of them.

"During class today, a teacher said something that if I said it, I would be fired."

"What did she say?"

"I don't really want to say, but a kid was acting up, and a Black female teacher made a comment to him."

"What did she say?"

"If I said it, I would be fired."

"What did she say?"

"She said, 'Sit your Black ass down.'"

Holding in a laugh, I said, "Did he sit down?"

"Yes."

"Did he begin working?"

"Yes."

"Did you want to say that to him?"

"No, but it's not right."

Of course, I said to the students that the teacher should have found another way to discipline that youngster, but in the back of my mind, I thought, *These white kids don't get it.* That teacher had a way of communicating with that young man. Though the teacher's words may seem crude, inappropriate, and even cruel to some, they were probably spoken with respect and love. Many of us have had parents or grandparents who might have said the same thing, using language these white students don't know and can't use. Their culture is different, and their mindset and experiences are all different. The graduate students were well-meaning, but the teacher had an innate relationship they couldn't replicate or fully understand. That said, the teacher probably should have addressed that child differently—or maybe not.

That is the point of this book. Black kids need Black adults who understand them and share a common language and history. They require teachers who can inspire, motivate, and discipline simultaneously. I contend—and this story will show—that the young people in their charge thrive whenever educators see themselves in their students' faces and vice versa.

Black people are beautiful, especially our children. We are an incredible people with a glorious history, an indelible style, and remarkable grace. Whenever I walk into a school and see the faces and movements of our children, I marvel at God's handiwork. Look at these precious children with their panache, promise, and brilliance. I see family, strength, resilience, possibilities, and our ancestors. I feel fortunate to be part of this incredible tribe of beautiful people!

I attended a workshop where the facilitator showed us a picture of a group of Black schoolchildren. She then asked each of us, "What do you see?" Many answers were given. No one said, "My children." She proposed, "How does the answer *my children* change the viewer's characterization of the picture?" Using the term *my children* implies an unyielding commitment. Seeing *my children* signifies a love and devotion that cannot be broken. I hurt when *my children* hurt, and I will do everything I can to see them prosper.

What do the people running and funding our schools see in that same picture? They would never condone failure if they could see these children as their own. They see the Black faces in the picture, but do they connect with them as they need to? I hear our children called "unfortunate," "underachievers," "level-one learners," and "at-risk students." I may not know exactly what school leaders see, but they can't think of these students as *my children* and allow them to fail. Do any of their own children attend schools with those faces? If so, school leaders wouldn't accept the poor results. They would fight and scream until things changed. The Banneker story shows what can happen when educators see *my children* in the faces of their students.

I primarily wrote this book as a tribute to the adults and students at Benjamin Banneker Academy for Community Development, where I served as principal from 1998 to 2008. Together, we created an exciting environment of Black culture and academic excellence—a vibrant and safe place for our children to learn and grow. I wanted to share how we accomplished that and, at the same time, recognize the efforts of all those involved. As you read the student quotations throughout this book, listen to what they say they gained by attending Banneker, then ask yourself if these are the types of students our community wants to develop. If so, shouldn't this approach be replicated nationwide in as many struggling schools as possible? Our society needs proud, educated Black children who become our next-generation leaders. Sadly, history has shown that this might not be what America wants.

They Were Black. All Black. is a meaningful tale of a high school in the Clinton Hill neighborhood of Brooklyn, New York. Banneker eventually had the highest graduation rate for Black students in New York State because it applied the principle that strong instruction driven by self-love and respect would lead to student success. It was integral that the adults saw *my children* in the classrooms.

The staff and students were predominantly African American. It should be noted that one's Blackness didn't automatically mean you had the correct perception of students, nor did being white automatically disqualify you, though race clearly played a factor. A running joke at our school was that you had to have locs to work at Banneker. That's not true, of course, but you did need to be aware of and respect Black identity and tradition.

> I remember my first week of Summer Bridge (2006); I kept observing all of my teachers in a surprising yet admiring way. I couldn't believe what I was seeing, so I kept quiet and waited until the following week to see if what I observed would change, but it didn't. My classmate then cracked a joke about what I'd been observing, "Excuse me, Ms. Matthews. Does every teacher in here have to have locks or natural hair?" The class started laughing, but I understood his question. I was fourteen years old, and I'd never been in a school where all the staff were Black and wore their natural hair. It changed my view and perspective of beauty and what was the norm. —S. Lawrence, Class of 2010

* * *

Throughout our history in America, Black teachers felt a familial, even ancestral, connection to their students and their future success. Early Black educators played a significant role in helping Banneker crystallize our mission. We created and cultivated a caring environment, much like the early segregated schools in the South. I looked to these early schools, established by newly freed Blacks, as a model. Their classrooms had dedicated, strong, no-nonsense educators with a crucial stake in student success. Historian Alvis Adair could easily be describing a Banneker teacher when he characterized the role of early African American teachers:

> Traditionally, the Black teacher has played multiple roles in schools. Among those have been teacher, parent, surrogate figure, counselor, disciplinarian, and modeling figure.

These roles have been anchored in a collective Black identity where these teachers perceive the success or failure
of their pupils as gains or losses to the Black community.
That is, the teacher and pupil share a common interest
and mission. The teachers view themselves as ethnically
responsible for preparing these youth for future leadership
and contributing to this unique mission, namely the lib-
eration and enhancement of the quality of life for Black
people.[2]

That is what our children need. All the other so-called
"solutions" to Black failure pale in comparison. Throughout my
many years in education, I have spoken to numerous principals
about school turnarounds. I made it clear that acquiring new
computers, new textbooks, new whiteboards, new curricula,
or any of the latest programs that so many schools pursue
will not help if you have inadequate teachers in front of your
students. I asked principals to examine who and what was in
the classrooms of the early segregated schools. Look at the
atmosphere, the seriousness, the no-nonsense dedication, the
love, the respect, and the commitment to success, exemplified
because the upliftment of the race was at stake. Those are
the essential ingredients that need to be firmly established,
and that comes from the character and resolve of dedicated
teachers. A few professional development sessions won't cut
it. Whatever was in those early, segregated classrooms is where
you should focus. Although the circumstances of these early
schools may appear very different from today's classrooms,
a culture was established that, if emulated, holds the key to
addressing today's Black student underachievement.

I think what made Banneker special was the strong sense
of community and Black pride that was throughout the
school. It wasn't forced. You genuinely felt the teachers

cared and wanted to advance the notion that Black children can succeed as long as people who look like them take the time and energy to invest in their future.
—K. Johnson, Class of 2013

* * *

I will not dwell on dismal statistics when it comes to Black underachievement and the learning gap. Sometimes, I think people like to hear those stats because they cement notions of Black inferiority. Researchers David Quinn and Tara-Marie Desruisseaux claim, "Despite long-standing efforts to close the achievement gap in education, the term [achievement gap] triggers racial stereotypes and causes a lower sense of urgency than when the issue is presented as the need to end inequality in educational outcomes."[3] The negative stats, though accurate, put the onus of failure on students. When the statistics say, "You are a level-one student," is the kid really a level-one student, or do the educators deserve that score? More than 60 percent of Black kids in New York City are not proficient in reading.[4] At face value, it seems something is wrong with the students. Educators must believe that students are not born at a level one. Students underachieve due to poor instruction, lack of adequate resources, and social inequities created by years of oppression. Race doesn't explain low achievement. Racism does!

There's a great deal of celebration when the proficiency of Black students increases by a few percentage points. That may be something to cheer about if these kids are not your children. As Black people, we must not be satisfied with mediocre test results that do not substantially shift the pendulum regarding learning and achievement for our students. We know the despair that follows when students of color do not get a quality education. Over 70 percent of the people incarcerated (in

U.S. prisons) didn't graduate from high school on time or at all.[5] According to the Hamilton Project, there is a 70 percent chance that an African American man without a high school diploma will be imprisoned before his thirty-first birthday.[6] The root cause of these issues can be directly traced back to the classroom.[7] When students of color are not educated adequately, they suffer disproportionately compared to their white counterparts. As a society, we must not accept these results because we know the promise and brilliance inside each Black student must be cultivated and supported.

In *They Were Black. All Black.* I make many references to the game of basketball. The sport was, and remains, an integral part of Black life. It has served as an outlet for Black expression, creativity, and leadership. In one school district where I worked, the top administrator stated that he didn't want students playing basketball; instead, he wanted them to focus on other activities. This was like telling James Brown, John Coltrane, or Prince to do something other than music. We should all be open to expanding our endeavors, but why downplay what makes us unique and special? It's like telling a Black person to straighten their hair, shrink the size of their nose, or reduce the size of their lips. Black people are extraordinary; so much of the world wants to emulate our swag and style.

I had an aunt who meant well, but she always told me to put the watermelon in a bag when coming from the grocery store. She was ashamed of our culture, who we were as Black people, and what we liked. Somehow, eating watermelon or carrying it for others to see was demeaning to her. We must celebrate all aspects of our culture: food, basketball, dancing, singing, storytelling, our traditions and legacies, our natural beauty and instinctive ways, our poetry, resilience, how we do church, and how we survived the brutality of our history.

THEY WERE BLACK. ALL BLACK.

Finally, the student quotations shared throughout the book are vital to *They Were Black. All Black.* I did not prompt any of the student responses included here. Using a survey, I asked one straightforward question: "What made the school special for you?" I did not canvas repeatedly for answers. One benefit of waiting ten years after I left the school to survey students was gaining a clear picture of how they progressed after graduation and hearing how they felt the school prepared them for their futures.

Hear their voices, digest their comments, and determine if their cultural development is as important as their academic achievements. Is there a causal relationship between the two?

Benjamin Banneker Academy will always hold a special place in my heart. I made lifelong friends here, met my future husband here, and had my Blackness affirmed and uplifted. Every day I came to school, I knew that I would be getting a quality education and that all of the faculty were fully invested in the success of all students. If I could relive my high school years, I would undoubtedly choose Banneker every single time. —A. Robinson, Class of 2007

Banneker was home for many reasons. Banneker embodied Black excellence, culture, and determination. The instructors met us where we were in our academics and helped us to reach our fullest potential. The clubs and activities were loving communities that helped us grow and mature into successful, well-rounded adults. Banneker could relate to every type of individual. —S. Jones, Class of 2005

Banneker is a community! The teachers made the experience special. The support was tough, motivating, and educationally fun. The push to make students understand fundamental values went above and beyond. Those values were instilled in me and in countless others of the Banneker community. The countless others are successful writers, creators, educators, entrepreneurs, politicians, activists, and respectful individuals within society. There was nothing like the Banneker experience! —I. Barrera, Class of 2007

Banneker was special because it was a safe space for Black teens to explore their diverse interests. It was also a norm to be cool, well-dressed, and have high grades. I remember sitting at the end of the halls on report card day, looking over my grades with my peers and strategizing how we were going to do even better the next term. —K. Croft, Class of 2013

Principal's Office, Benjamin Banneker High School, Brooklyn, New York

October 10, 2000

Rock: Hey Coach, I see a lot of kids signed up for tryouts.

Coach: About one hundred boys showed up. The gym was packed.

Rock: Black kids love basketball.

Coach: Yeah, Rock, Black kids love this game. Think I'll dress about fifteen kids on Varsity and maybe another twenty-five on JV.

Rock: Damn, that many. That's good.

Coach: Our kids need to be around Black men, and our coaches can help.

Rock: Yeah, when I coached in high school, I felt that bond with the kids. It is as strong a bond as that between a parent and a child. Believe me, Saunders, I influenced a lot more kids coaching basketball than I did when I was teaching them in math class. What are we going to do about all the other kids who don't make it?

Coach: Let's set up an intramural program for the kids who don't make it.

Rock: Good idea! Okay, let me know how much that would cost, Coach. Think I will expand the program so more kids get to play, not just Varsity or JV. We have to find a way to get more kids playing—boys and girls. Talk to Mr. G, the dean, about setting up the program.

Coach: Yeah, okay. Mr. G has developed a basketball program called *Work Hard Play Hard* at other places. We can bring that here.

Rock: I saw the girls' team tryouts. They look like they will also be strong this year. They have a good coach.

Coach: Yeah, Rock, she is strong. We've been going back and forth about gym practice time.

Rock: Girls are getting on me for not showing them enough love and getting to more of their games.

Coach: You don't mind us having these weekly conversations, do you, Rock?

Rock: No, I appreciate them. Gives me a chance to talk about the team. One thing I missed about leaving teaching and becoming a principal was giving up coaching basketball. I loved it. Any word about Gary, Coach?

Coach: No.

2

MY JOURNEY

I was born and raised in Brooklyn and attended public schools through high school. My first job after college was tutoring middle and elementary school students at Siloam Presbyterian Church in Brooklyn, New York. I knew right away that teaching was my calling. I taught math at a middle school for eight years and at a high school for ten years before becoming an assistant principal, principal, and then a superintendent. I also worked as an adjunct math professor at Medgar Evers College, New York University, Hunter College, and Virginia State University. This book is not, per se, an autobiography, but I will share two of my life experiences that played significant roles in shaping the educational approach I brought to Benjamin Banneker Academy.

* * *

FIRST DAY OF MIDDLE SCHOOL

If you ask them, most people of color remember the first time they experienced racial hatred on a guttural level. Most will never forget because it has such a profound impact. It's one thing to see images on television or in movies or read about racism, but it is very different when you experience it first-hand. That first racist encounter stings and stays with you, becoming part of your DNA if you're not careful.

It was the first day of junior high school at JHS 62. I was thirteen years old. Like most thirteen-year-olds, I often saw anger: kids fighting, drivers on the road yelling at each other, onscreen disputes, and family arguments. These were all part of my early experiences. However, they all paled when I experienced racial malice up close for the very first time. Strangely, it wasn't even directed at me but at another student. It was an exchange I never forgot, marking the beginning of my journey to Banneker.

My junior high was in a mostly white neighborhood. My family had recently moved there, mainly to escape crime and bad schools. All the seventh graders seemed nervous that first day. There were about five hundred students in my grade. Only about thirty of us were Black, and there were no Black teachers. My homeroom class had three Black students. One of them, Concho, remains one of my closest friends. I am the godfather to his kids.

A presentation was held in the auditorium for all the new students. The older kids were putting on a show, and it was funny. I sat behind Tyrone, a Black student, laughing at the performance and feeling less anxious about being in a new school. Tyrone asked me when the show would end because he had to catch his bus. We were sitting by the aisle. He tapped the arm of a white male teacher standing in the aisle. The teacher responded, "Don't you ever put your nasty, filthy, dirty hands on me." Tyrone slumped back in his chair, defeated, but I don't think he felt as bad as I did. I felt the teacher was speaking to every Black kid in that auditorium, including me. He was so venomous. It was as if he were talking to an animal. I looked at that teacher and saw that this wasn't about simple annoyance or even anger, but a deeply seated racial hatred. I'd never seen anyone, unprovoked, speak to a child like that. I never forgot that experience and couldn't enjoy the rest of the show.

I watched this teacher as he walked around the auditorium. I saw him interact with the other teachers and noticed them laughing and joking. In my seventh-grade mind, they were all conspiring and all guilty of racial hatred. I don't remember this teacher's name; I never had him as a teacher, but I can see his face just as clearly today as I did in the seventies. As tears welled in my eyes, I asked myself, *Why am I at this school? Why do we need to leave our neighborhood to find good schools? Why can't we be in our schools with people who care about us and want us to be there?*

This ugly, racial experience has been my driving force throughout my educational journey. That question—*Why do we have to leave our neighborhood?* —led me to Banneker. I wanted to be part of a model that demonstrated we don't need to attend *their* schools to get a good education. This was my dream, my motivation, my passion, my mission: a school in our neighborhood where Black children felt safe and free from bigotry, ugliness, mean-spiritedness, and racial animus.

Despite this early traumatizing event, I had a great time at that middle school. I made lifelong friends and got a decent education. However, I learned very little about Black culture and history. I got that from home. I remember my mother once coming to school to straighten out a white teacher who had given me a poor grade on a report that I had written about Malcolm X. My mother made it clear to that teacher that I was capable of choosing my heroes, and she shouldn't judge my paper based on her beliefs. That teacher changed my grade. Despite white students throwing rocks at us or calling us names, my friends and I came together as a group and became emboldened. We did everything together—ate in the cafeteria, played basketball, and socialized. One fortuitous outcome of integration is that it often brought people of color closer together.

During my time at JHS 62, I encountered white teachers who were racist and dismissive, but a few were warm and tried to make us feel welcome. I remember them fondly, and when I became a new teacher, I incorporated some of the pedagogical skills I observed. Despite the few well-meaning white teachers, there was a general feeling that Black kids didn't belong there. The fact that most of us were bused in further stigmatized us. But, as I mentioned earlier, this book is not about criticizing white teachers. That isn't helpful, yet it must be pointed out that it takes more than well-meaning white teachers to turn things around for Black children. Our kids need support and care from teachers who look like them and uplift the rich culture and history left by ancestors who expect advancement and excellence as the generations progress.

Throughout my lengthy career as an educator, I never forgot the dream of a school for our kids in our neighborhood, taught by loving teachers who held high standards for the personal and collective achievements of the students in their charge.

> What can I say? Banneker was a TRUE family. There was never a day that I didn't feel safe in that school. When the world was harsh and cruel, Banneker loved me. I was able to gain the truest of friendships there. The biggest takeaway was that Rock and the staff instilled greatness and fostered a strong resilience in me. We were taught about the power we possessed. Banneker truly bred warriors. We were taught that we were special and were treated that way, too. —C. Hudson, Class of 2008

This school was truly transformative for me. The life lessons I learned attending Benjamin Banneker were just as plentiful as the schoolwork I was taught. At every turn within 77 Clinton Avenue, I felt embraced, and it was the first time in my life that I was genuinely welcomed and encouraged to believe in myself, my intelligence, my young womanhood, and my Blackness in a school setting. I was praised when I succeeded, and I was disciplined and corrected with love even when I fell short. I'd never attended a school until Benjamin Banneker, where I felt every single staff member had my best interest at heart, truly got to know me as a person, and wanted to see me win. I've never attended a school where simply walking into the building gave me a sense of comfort and safety. Attending school every day felt like leaving my family at home to see my family at school. —D. Stewart, Class of 2009

*　*　*

BASKETBALL ADVICE

I had just been selected to teach at a high school in Brooklyn. The person who placed me there was one of the few African Americans working at the Department of Education at the time, and he asked me where I wanted to teach. "Any school?" I asked. He replied, "Yes, and when you go there, don't let them tell you there are no vacancies." I went to my top choice. When they saw me, they said they had no openings. I insisted they call downtown because I was told they had an opening for a math teacher.

The principal and the assistant principal took me to the office and asked me to do some simple math problems. *Stop and Frisk.* The quiz happened even though I had a high school math license and a master's degree. I got the job, becoming one of seven Black teachers in a school with 220 teachers.

On the elevator on my first day, a white man got on and said, "Hey, you look like you know basketball. Do you work here?" I said, "Yeah." He said, "I am the athletic director, and we need a coach. Are you interested?" Now, here I was, a teacher with a master's degree in math, ready to do high-level mathematics, but this white guy asked me about basketball. At first, I was insulted, but I did love basketball. The job was after school. I took the assignment, assembled a team, and began regular practices and games during that first year.

I coached by the seat of my pants. I played and watched many basketball games and knew how to teach, so I thought I was ready. We had a terrible first season, winning only two games.

I was determined to do better the following year. I read books, watched tapes, and attended coaching clinics. At one of those clinics, a well-known coach emphasized *pressure defense*. For those who aren't basketball fanatics, this means playing tough defense and making it difficult for the other team to advance the ball up the court. I liked it a lot. It was fast, and our kids would enjoy the quick pace and spontaneity it brought. I listened to every word this coach said and copied all the diagrams as he spoke passionately about this defensive strategy. I was ready that October.

At every practice session, we reviewed pressure defense, where each player should be, and how to react. We worked on this strategy incessantly, but our second season wasn't much better than the first. We only won five games.

After that season, I attended another basketball clinic to learn more about pressure defense. The same expert was there again, and we explored the nuances of this strategy once more. After his seminar, he spoke with some of us who had attended the clinic the previous year. We asked more questions about this defense.

I told him that our team had a disappointing year after using this tactic, but we were committed to getting better next year. I asked him what we should focus on, and he hesitated for a minute.

"Look, if you want to be successful coaches, focus on getting players who can jump, run, and shoot," he told us.

"What about the pressure defense?" we asked.

"Strategies are one thing, but they don't matter in the long run. The athlete's ability is what's going to make the difference," he said. "Get some good players, and you will be just fine."

I recruited better players the next year and never had a losing season after that. One year, we only lost one game.

The lesson learned was more important than winning games. This advice was one of the best I'd ever heard and contributed to my leadership success at Banneker. I gained more insight from a respected basketball coach's guidance than from the leadership courses I completed in graduate school. The coach told me that all the strategies in the world wouldn't ensure my success as a leader. Organizations need talented individuals with strong skills. A leader's role is to identify the best people, bring them on board, and let go of those who are not competent.

Doc Rivers, basketball coach for the Boston Celtics, lost fifty-eight out of eighty games one year, and the following year won the championship. Did he become a better coach the following year, or was it that the team acquired Ray Allen and Kevin Garnett, two of the best NBA players at the time? Principals must find excellent teachers, like a basketball coach who finds top athletes. We must find and recruit teachers with the skills to teach Black children. I became an effective principal when I went out and found the best teachers for our children.

Think about a positive K-12 experience you had as a student. Does it involve a special teacher? Many times, it does.

The same goes for a negative experience. The teacher was the focal point. The critical variable is always the person who stands in front of the students, not the curriculum, textbooks, or smart boards. It's never new strategies or technology, but the teacher in the classroom.

Throughout my teaching career, I found many of my colleagues to be mean-spirited, boring, dismissive, and racially biased, and some clearly should not have been in the classroom. I remember being an assistant principal at a high school with about forty math teachers. When I left to become a principal, someone asked which teachers I would bring to my new assignment if I could, and I said, "None of them." They were not competent and were ill-equipped to teach children, specifically Black children. Some were better than others, but ultimately, they could not motivate, inspire, or discipline our students. Most of these colleagues were white, but the Black teachers at this school were not great either. Our children deserve and need the best teachers, and administrators must prioritize providing quality teachers if our students are to succeed in school and beyond.

Benjamin Banneker was… is special to me because I knew every single teacher believed in me, believed in us. From the very first day of school, each teacher spoke to freshmen about college. We were constantly being prepared. Of course, we didn't always appreciate it, but I don't think I would be who I am today if it weren't for the teachers and mentors I had at Banneker. I didn't go to an HBCU like many of my peers, but going to Banneker felt like an HBCU. It felt like a community of celebrated Blackness. We felt empowered and intelligent, and we were constantly being reminded that our lives had value. Before the term "Black Lives Matter" became so commonplace, Banneker taught me that Black lives mattered through the actions of its teachers and the education they provided. —N. Steadman, Class of 2001

I felt so proud to be African American. I felt like I belonged; I felt special as a student. I remember getting so much support as a student. I experienced so many challenges and always received support. I remember my uncle passing away while I was a student; I went to school the next day because I had to study for the Regents, and one of the Banneker staff members noticed a change in my mood right away and provided me with so much support. I felt supported and loved by all Banneker staff members. I appreciate this school so much, especially Mr. Egashira, one of my English teachers, who highlighted my writing strengths and taught me so much about African American history. —N. Peters, Class of 2009

DARYL ROCK

Principal's Office, Benjamin Banneker High School, Brooklyn, New York

October 24, 2000

Rock: I looked in on your first practice, Coach. Team looks good. But, damn, if we had Gary.

Coach: I know, but he is gone.

Rock: Still haven't heard from him?

Coach: No, and his school is only a few blocks away. Our other coaches feel a little disrespected, but I understand his decision.

Rock: Looks like Kareem will have to step up and be the man then, Coach.

Coach: We are going to post him up a lot.

Rock: Kareem needs to work on that drop step.

Coach: We work with him every day. He's very coachable.

Rock: Andy is looking good, also. Saw the first scrimmage. Our guys have a lot of energy. You need to take it easy arguing with the refs, though, Coach. You will not make it through the first week of the season that way.

Coach: You're right. I get too excited.

Rock: Didn't you pull that Bobby Knight trick, throwing a chair, last year?

Coach: Yeah, but I am more relaxed this year.

Rock: Didn't look like it at the scrimmage. Why are you so calm and mellow off the court, but get hyped up during practice and games?

Coach: Black passion, I guess.

Rock: How well do you know Gordon, the Black ref? I remember when I was coaching, and he did one of our games, and a kid from the other team pulled a gun on him during the game.

Coach: Get out of here, Rock.

Rock: Yes, during the game! The kid ran to his backpack, pulled out a pistol, and his coach and athletic director tackled him.

Coach: Did they call the cops?

Rock: No, but we did. You know Coach Richard Barclift.

Coach: Yeah, Bard.

Rock: He was the assistant coach, and he called the cops, and we got out of there. Didn't even change out of our uniforms—just jetted. They had the nerve to be mad at me for ending the game. That ref never budged. Just stood on the court the whole time. He's got a lot of courage or is just crazy.

Coach: Wow, that's wild, Rock.

Rock: Saw that you have the guys doing a lot of trapping. That's the way you are going to play this year?

Coach: Mostly half-court traps—a one-three-one with Kareem on the back line.

Rock: Is he fast enough?

Coach: He is.

Rock: He is gonna be playing with a lot of young kids. Can he handle the pressure?

Coach: He is showing leadership skills and should be okay if he doesn't try to do too much.

Rock: Are there any academic problems, Coach? We are going by the book. We don't want to play anyone who is not eligible. Remember, we had that issue a couple of years ago when we had to forfeit games because a player wasn't eligible.

Coach: No, we are not having any of that drama. You will see all the report cards. Students must pass all major classes.

Rock: Saw the girls' first practice the other day. I really like their new coach. Are you getting along with each other?

Coach: We negotiated a gym schedule. They are serious and practice every day. They have some pretty good players.

Rock: Can you believe a fifteen-year-old kid was going to shoot a referee on the court because he didn't like the ref's calls? We have a lot of work to do with our children.

Coach: You got that right.

3

OUR PHILOSOPHICAL APPROACH

When speaking to people about my high school experience, I always say Benjamin Banneker was like a Historically Black High School. It was very Afrocentric and community-oriented, always pushing the narrative of the importance of Black history and Black achievement. During a pivotal time when a teenager is learning the value of mentorship, developing friendships that will last into adulthood, learning about their favorite subjects that will mold into careers, and learning the importance of Black excellence along the way is an experience. And I cherish having had that experience to this day. I jokingly say that there's a chip that's activated in alumni years after we graduate. A chip that helps us realize the relevance and value of being taught resilience, being unapologetically Black, and staying true to our roots and our community. I'm forever grateful and proud to be a Benjamin Banneker Warrior.

—S. Lawrence, Class of 2010

Benjamin Banneker integrated educational philosophies and practices used by early segregated school administrators in the South, who were successful in educating oppressed and deprived African American students. At Banneker, we discovered that the same spirit and "dogged determination" that surmounted many of the educational roadblocks in the nineteenth century can be effectively applied to educate our students in the twenty-first century, thoroughly preparing them for future success.

After the Civil War, the task of providing public education to newly emancipated African Americans living in the Southern United States fell mainly to the Black community itself. With the temporary financial and organizational assistance of the Freedmen's Bureau, along with philanthropic, religious, and instructional support from white Northerners, many local African American teachers assumed the responsibility of educating their own community.[8] According to the National Archives, the Freedmen's Bureau "helped freed people establish schools, purchase land, locate family members, and legalize marriages. The Bureau also supplied necessities such as food and clothing, operated hospitals and temporary camps, and witnessed labor contracts between freedmen and plantation owners or other employers."[9]

Once the Bureau had been disbanded after seven years, Southern white leaders furthered discriminatory philosophies and social practices using their political and economic clout to negatively affect Black educational opportunities. The South's segregated schools led to the inequitable disbursement of public education funds; more money was allocated to white schools and programs than to African American schools. As a result, learning institutions for African Americans were housed in inadequate school facilities and lacked adequately trained teachers. Books, furniture, educational supplies, and other learning resources were also scarce and limited. Parental and community support for formal education was sometimes challenging to obtain, resulting in low school attendance. Many students were required to work to help support their families or care for younger siblings who were not yet school age.[10]

These factors ultimately affected the literacy and overall learning levels of Black students. Despite these impediments, educators teaching in segregated schools in the South, along with the students themselves, understood the importance and value of education. Teachers sought and secured appropriate training, donated their time, and helped raise funds to purchase equipment and supplies, thereby improving the condition of their schools. They served as mentors, representatives, liaisons, information providers, and cultural keepers for their students, schools, and communities.

Although these early Southern segregated schools for African American students were poorly funded and had few resources, evidence suggests that the environment had effective traits, particularly institutional policies and community support, that helped African American children learn despite segregation, discrimination, and neglect.[11] Author Thomas Sowell states, "The schools are remembered as having an atmosphere where support, encouragement, and rigid standards combined to enhance students' self-worth and increase their aspirations to achieve."[12]

I remember my grandmother talking about the one-room schoolhouse she went to as a child. It was crowded with students of all ages and skill levels, with a pot-bellied stove in the middle of the room. There was usually a stern teacher she admired. She often said matter-of-factly, "We couldn't attend the white school," as if that was her permanent station in life. Her acceptance of segregation felt hurtful to me, but hearing how she fondly remembered learning to read and write at the "colored school" with a wonderful teacher was enlightening and inspiring.

Dr. Lester Young, Superintendent of District 13, shared a copy of *Their Highest Potential*, a book that greatly influenced my growth as an educator. Vanessa Walker describes these early schools as community-valued schooling. Banneker exemplified this blend of support, high standards, and a nurturing community spirit. This core philosophy has significantly contributed to our school's success.

Securing skilled, caring, and resourceful teachers was a top priority at Banneker, and achieving this contributed to our academic success. The teachers in the early schools were mainly female, very bright, no-nonsense, and determined. They understood their students' backgrounds and kept them actively involved in learning while maintaining authority and showing compassion. These early teachers faced many challenges but remained dedicated to their students and their mission. In *Their Highest Potential*, one student described her teacher: "She would always tell you wherever you went, always feel that you are important, that you are somebody. And she made every child in the room feel that way."[13] That student could have been describing a Banneker teacher.

After four years of my principalship, Banneker students received that same message from their teachers. This was evident whenever I walked into any classroom, but getting to that point took a great deal of work.

It takes a village to raise a child. Banneker was my village. The heart of Banneker was "family," and it was a safe space for learning and personal development. It was a school that understood the nuances of being a Black student in the New York City public school system, and it wanted to provide each child with broader opportunities and a top-tier education. I believed I could be and achieve anything because I had a support system of teachers, leaders, and faculty who empowered me, believed in me before I believed in myself, and reminded me to be proud of my culture and who I am as a young Black woman. I synonymized Black with "excellence" at an early age because I witnessed it on a daily basis throughout the classroom and halls. —J. Daniel, Class of 2003

Principal's Office, Benjamin Banneker High School, Brooklyn, New York

October 25, 2000

Rock: Hey, Coach. I saw Gary today.

Coach: Get out of here.

Rock: He was here at the school. Came into my office looking all down and out. I asked him how things were going. He said, "Okay," but I could tell something was not right. I said, "You miss your Banneker family, don't you?" He kinda looked like he was ashamed of his decision to leave. We sat and talked for a little while, then I told him half-jokingly, "If you want to come back, all you need to do is have your mother come up to the school, and we can sign you back in."

Coach: If you think about it, Rock, it's probably best for him to stay where he is. He will play against stronger competition and get more recognition. He will practice every day against tougher players. More college coaches will see him. Why would he come back to our small school? Plus, his friends and family were pushing him to leave.

Rock: I think he misses our family, Coach. I could see the look on his face. Are your coaches ever going to forgive him?

Coach: I don't know. We trained him, worked with him, showed him love, and he just got up and left us without any warning.

Rock: He is still a good kid and will always be part of Banneker.

Coach: Yeah, you're right. He is a great kid.

4

IT'S THE TEACHERS!

Banneker valued Black excellence. Banneker taught us that Black Lives Matter before it was a movement. Banneker was the school that taught us, as young Black leaders, that we have magic running through our veins. Banneker taught us how to love each other, how to stick together, and how to give back to our community. We had teachers who loved us and made that known. We had teachers who paved the way for us to be the change-makers we are today. This allowed us to stand on their backs and be the leaders we are today. People didn't understand how it felt to walk through those doors every day. Banneker was MONUMENTAL in my life. It made me who I am today.

—E. Braithwaite, Class of 2009

When I arrived at Banneker, I was excited to see that almost all the teachers and administrators were Black. It was uplifting to walk into a building filled with Afrocentric posters and artifacts everywhere. Although the students at every school I had worked at before Banneker were mainly Black, the staff was mostly white. Banneker was Black!

Ms. Davidson, the co-principal, and I conducted classroom walk-throughs during my first two weeks. To my surprise, about a quarter of the teachers were excellent. Another 15 percent were okay; sadly, the rest were not good. Some had no presence in the classroom. Others were unfamiliar with the content, and many didn't like the kids. Students were often bored and combative in those classrooms, which led to unruliness that carried over into the hallways and other classes. One math teacher, held in high esteem, spoke to the blackboard throughout the entire lesson. Other teachers were unprepared and tried to wing their lessons. The worst teachers showed utter contempt for the students. I always wondered why anyone would teach if they didn't like kids.

The great teachers were exceptional, some of the best educators I've ever seen. However, many others were ineffective, and they shaped the school's culture. When people in a school behave poorly, they influence everyone. This could be the janitor, counselors, teachers, PTA members, or security guards. It doesn't matter who they are. They need to change their behavior or leave. For the record, changing people's behavior is very difficult.

I knew we needed to replace the ineffective teachers. Superintendent Dr. Young and the district administration supported me as we implemented significant changes. It became clear that the teachers who were not capable felt threatened and uneasy. At first, I didn't discipline anyone, but when they observed how I engaged with students and parents, they understood I held high expectations for everyone. I was dedicated to ensuring our students received the best education possible. Poor instruction would not be accepted. It was clear in my daily interactions that I deeply valued the seriousness of education and the importance of doing it right.

After my first six months, nearly half of the teachers submitted a petition to the superintendent criticizing my leadership. They aimed to keep the status quo. Making personnel changes is the most difficult part of a principal's job. How can you create meaningful change without causing some kind of uprising? To this day, I remember every name on that list. Only one of the top teachers signed that letter. High expectations do not threaten good teachers, so I didn't expect to see many of the excellent teachers' names on that list of disgruntled staff.

Things weren't good during those months. I remember graduation day that year, when some teachers were grading the math finals in the cafeteria, and I was helping. Eight teachers were in the room, and the radio was on while we marked the exams. After grading for about an hour, a teacher approached me and asked, "Are you listening to the radio?" I started listening and couldn't believe what I was hearing. The disgruntled Banneker teachers who created the petition were guests on a radio talk show. They were bad-mouthing me terribly. Though it was humiliating, I decided then that they would not win. It stressed me out a bit, and my graduation speech wasn't my best. However, those teachers gave me fuel to charge forward.

We were now in an all-out war—not so much between the teachers and me, but between the kids and them, with me leading the charge. Like Malcolm X said, "If you have no critics, you'll likely have no success."[14] I was fired up, but I knew I had to be cautious.

As I now tell principals, when you need to replace teachers, you can't try to remove all of them at once. Doing so will most likely cause a rebellion from which you might not recover. Target the worst offenders carefully. Everyone in the school knows who they are, and most teachers won't feel threatened because they don't see themselves as part of *the problem*. Strong teachers might be friends with less competent ones, but most excellent teachers don't want to support anyone who weakens the school. The top teachers were on our side, and the dissenters were losing allies and starting to feel isolated. They realized I wasn't going away, and I could win this fight. The parents knew I was on their side, advocating for their children, and they supported me. Parental and community allies became my greatest assets.

After my first year, four or five teachers left. You can't imagine what a difference this made. Consistent write-ups and poor classroom evaluations sped up their exits. I would sit daily in classrooms with weak instructors, pointing out problem areas. If they were late, I recorded that. I would hold them accountable if they didn't have clear lesson plans. I spent countless hours writing reports and attending teacher union conferences. As expected, some teachers wanted to avoid this scrutiny and left of their own accord. With new openings, we had a chance to bring in more qualified teachers dedicated to our students' educational success. This is like subtracting a negative number in math. By taking them away, you are in essence adding.

We replaced five or six more teachers in my second year, and the atmosphere began to feel noticeably different. By my fourth year, all the malcontents had left, and you could walk into any classroom and see effective teaching. The battle was over, but reaching that end wasn't easy. There were many hearings, union grievances, mini revolts, and sleepless nights, but the students kept me motivated. I stayed firmly committed to them and their futures. I attended so many grievance hearings that the arbitrators all knew me by name. This is the grind many leaders avoid, but it is necessary. I was not surrendering. There was just too much at stake.

In those early years, students would come to my office and tell me what was happening in the classrooms. They were almost always right. There was a lot of dysfunction occurring. *School leaders must act decisively in the face of incompetence!* Would you keep a player on your basketball team if they consistently threw the ball away, missed shots, or dribbled the ball off their feet? You would ultimately have no choice but to replace that player. If you had a business and a salesperson wasn't meeting their quota quarter after quarter, costing you money, would you keep them? Why do we think it's acceptable to keep incompetent teachers who produce failing students? Parents complained, but too often, the kids had no one to advocate for them.

A few years after I retired from Banneker, I recall sitting in the back of one of my graduate students' middle school math classrooms. I wore a suit and tie as complete chaos unfolded around me. Interestingly, the students ignored me, the stranger in the back, and they kept spewing expletives. Usually, I avoid intervening during ineffective lessons at schools where I'm not employed. This way, I don't risk undermining the teacher. Although tempted, I said nothing to try to get the students under control. I noticed another woman was in the classroom during the lesson. I assumed she was a paraprofessional. After a while, a young Latina girl turned around, looked at me, not knowing who I was, and quietly said, "Please help us to learn." I didn't know what to say because I had no authority in that classroom, that building, or within the district. It was a sad moment for me.

Who will help or save our students from this situation if not the leaders? These chaotic, out-of-control classrooms exist across the country. Our children deserve better.

After the class, I asked the graduate student, "Who was the woman sitting in the room during the lesson?" Imagine my shock when my student replied, "She is the principal." What? *How does a principal allow such drama without interrupting the chaos, and why is the young girl asking me for help with her principal sitting right there?* Something was very wrong!

Of course, some teachers need support. Most new teachers require a lot of support, and they received it at Banneker. We were patient with new teachers, understanding they would likely struggle at first. Most novice teachers are unprepared for a classroom of thirty students with agendas different from their own. We allowed for some failures and continued to nurture teachers through the process, but we also knew teachers needed to work out some issues independently. Many struggled during the first term, but we could tell which teachers would eventually succeed. The first interview with a new teacher revealed their energy, determination, consciousness, and willingness to learn and improve. We had many young teachers, many of whom were Black males. When selecting teachers, we looked for that one crucial trait: character, which is almost impossible to develop.

Co-principal Davidson had a wonderful way of giving constructive feedback when she worked with our teachers. She saw the teachers as family, and they valued her caring approach. We worked well together. I managed conflicts with the teachers, and she helped new teachers establish a positive school culture.

The first interview question I asked potential teachers was, "Why are Black children so far behind in school?" Teachers responded with a variety of reasons: poverty, drug use, neglectful parents, racism, rap music, slow learners being passed along, lack of resources, lack of discipline, and the media—all valid explanations for student failure, but not what I was looking for.

Occasionally, a teacher candidate would say, "It was because they didn't get good instruction." Hired! That answer signaled they believed students of color could succeed with quality teaching despite many obstacles. They believed that with proper instruction, young Black kids could attain success, and they were willing to be held accountable—no ready-made excuses.

Think about that for a moment: if you believe that some factor other than yourself causes failure, then when things go wrong, you can claim it wasn't your fault; it was due to the circumstances. Teachers must believe that children who receive good instruction can succeed, and as their teacher, *I can be the one to make it happen.*

Upon entering the school building, the teacher's belief system is most essential, not whether one can write a clear lesson plan, put up a bulletin board, or pace instruction effectively. You can *train* someone to do those things, but you can't train a teacher to look at Black children and see them as *my children.* Professional development can't change a person's belief system. Schools can try to retrain adults, but they will still see Black children the same way they always have and, as a result, will relate to them based on that belief system. Black children need adults who see them as family and have the character and will to move students forward.

That was our approach at Banneker, and it should be the same for schools aiming to advance Black children. Helen Keller, the disability activist, once said, "Character cannot be developed in ease and quiet. Only through the experience of trial and suffering can the soul be strengthened, vision cleared, ambition inspired, and success achieved."[15] Those who understand and feel the struggles Black people have endured have built the character needed to teach Black children. That's what the early Black educators had, what the Banneker teachers had, and what contributed to our success.

Due to this mindset, teacher recruitment became my main focus as principal. My strongest administrative skill was judging character. Finding outstanding teachers required effort. I made a point to attend every job fair in the area, as well as some outside the state. I built relationships with local colleges and visited classrooms of graduating students majoring in education. The professors always welcomed me, and I talked to their students about what it takes to become a successful teacher. At the same time, I recruited those students who showed promise.

Additionally, the district's human resources staff knew me, and whenever a new teacher who met our criteria came to their attention, they would contact me. Some teachers transferred from other schools, but most were homegrown. Recruitment was ongoing. We understood that some teachers would leave for administrative positions or other reasons, and we would need to fill those vacancies.

Many of the teachers I hired came directly from college. If we saw potential in a new candidate, I would hire them even if their major wasn't in education. I would bring them on, and during their early years of teaching, they could return to school and get certified. During my tenure, the certification requirements changed. In many states, including New York, certification is now required before beginning a teaching position. Although well-meaning, the new teacher certification rules made it more difficult for us to hire young teachers. Think about it—what does certification really mean? Does it mean you can communicate effectively with students of color? Does it mean you respect their parents? Does it mean you genuinely like these young people? Does it mean you are not afraid of them? No, it simply means you know how to write a lesson plan and are familiar with some scholars who have developed educational philosophies. Those academics might be interesting, but you need more than that to teach Black kids.

I hired Ms. Richmond, a teacher lacking teaching experience or education credits. She walked into the school one day after recently graduating from college and said, "I would like to be a teacher here." She looked like one of our students. We interviewed her, and we hired her on the spot. In her first year, she faced some challenges with classroom management. She was receptive to support and eventually figured it out. She ultimately developed a teaching style that was truly remarkable to see. Her rapport with the students was excellent, and her students achieved high scores on the Regents exams. She became a master teacher, and when she left the school after six years to pursue her PhD, she had not yet completed her certification, yet she was one of the best history teachers I had ever seen.

At Banneker, we had a good mix of veteran and novice teachers. Many experienced staff volunteered to mentor new teachers without a formal peer support system. Seasoned teachers naturally assisted newer colleagues, much like helping a younger sibling or cousin. That's what family does. We had formal staff development in place but kept it to a minimum. Teachers had different styles, and when those styles were effective, we didn't push them to adopt new techniques. However, we made it clear that, as professionals, they needed to stay up to date with new educational approaches. They didn't have to implement them, but they needed to be mindful of them. Teaching is largely an art; artists need the freedom to practice their craft. Some teachers ran teacher-centered classes, while others focused more on students. I preferred a more student-centered classroom, but some of our best teachers stood at the front and directed lessons where all students hung on every word. Why would I ask them to change their technique when it clearly benefited student learning? I aimed to visit each teacher's classroom every day for a minute or two. I asked myself whether students were engaged and whether teachers were preparing them for the standards set by the state. Many classrooms had lively discussions about current issues not on the curriculum, and that was fine. Still, we understood that if we didn't prepare students to meet certain standards, we'd be doing them a disservice. They had to take the Regents exams,

New York State's version of final exams, and it was the teachers' responsibility to ensure their students passed. We acknowledge that standardized tests aren't always the best measures of student learning; however, because they are required, we owe it to our students to prepare them thoroughly. Fighting the use of standardized tests wasn't a battle we were willing to fight. We needed to help our students graduate on time and prepare for college.

In summary, if we want to make an impact, we must develop strong teachers by:

(a) Recruiting students as young as middle school to encourage their involvement in teaching.
(b) Sending young contemporary recruiters to encourage Black college students to pursue teaching careers while demonstrating that teachers don't have to be drab and corny but can be stylish and cool.
(c) Increasing salary and housing incentives. (Where can New York City teachers live with the high costs of renting or purchasing a home?)
(d) Attending HBCUs and offering scholarships to students with engaging personalities who can inspire and motivate young people. Let these college students begin tutoring to see if they are comfortable working with children. Determine whether they embody a sense of pride regarding Black people and our history in America.

We can find and develop these warrior teachers if we love our children. We found them for Banneker, and I believe all school administrators can find quality teachers if they have the resolve to change the trajectory for Black youth in America.

Walking through those doors every day felt like home. Our teachers were aunts and uncles. Admins were second parents. There was always an immense amount of love and understanding that came from everyone. We have formed bonds that people say only happen in college. My close friends, my child's godparents, and my career mentors all came from Benjamin Banneker. —D. Dekattu, Class of 2007

The permeating, underlying sentiment of family was the motivating factor for faculty, staff, and students during my years there. We were all dedicated to making an impact on the lives of the greatest young minds the world has ever seen. The kids, however, may have impacted our lives even more than we did theirs. As staff members, we had to be better in our roles and responsibilities because of what was at stake. It forced every one of us, at every position, to edify ourselves on how to be more effective. The children were counting on us to be the best version of ourselves, and we refused to let them down. —T. Tuggle, Assistant Dean

The faculty at Benjamin Banneker *made* the school! I know students would credit their success to the faculty. I do. —L. James, Class of 2013

I worked at Banneker for over fifteen years, and it was one of the best schools for African American and other students of color because of the staff, parents, and students. Most were highly motivated to convey the importance of African history to the diaspora. Every subject was a nourishing environment that expressed the belief of our rich history, which included both achievements and struggles. Banneker was a powerful, Afrocentric family that just happened to exist in a school building. Students, faculty, and parents spent hours together after school. It was a safe haven for all, where at times "school" started at 3:00 p.m. On many occasions, our Banneker family didn't leave the building till 9:00 p.m. or later. Banneker was filled with guidance, laughter, joy, knowledge, and most of all, a community that cared, not only for each other, but for the community at large. —V. Ellis, Staff, 2008

* * *

By now, it should be clear that my philosophical approach to education is that teachers and other adults make or break the school experience for children. Nothing else really matters. I have had the chance to visit many schools across the country, and sadly, wherever you find Black children, too often, you see struggling schools with poor instruction. As I walked through these schools, classroom after classroom, I saw inadequate and uninspired teaching, where teachers were so dull that students slept, or where students were allowed to turn the classroom into chaos and frivolity. Many classes were completely out of control, and where there was some structure, students were engaged in busywork that didn't meet state standards.

Then, undoubtedly, it would happen. I'd walk into a classroom where vibrant instruction was happening. Students were engaged in discussions and work, and the room felt alive. Educators know what I'm referring to. It's a classroom full of hope and promise amidst a sea of dysfunction and chaos in the larger school building.

Which variables change when effective teaching is present in the classroom? After all, they were the same students, parents, poverty levels, lack of resources, and neighborhoods. What's different is the teacher! The person in front of those students makes all the difference. *Every educational leader needs to understand that students in their school are failing because they don't have excellent teachers*! It's your responsibility to ensure your kids have the best teachers. Period.

I remember my first year teaching at a middle school in the Bushwick section of Brooklyn, NY. I was young and inexperienced, and most of my classes were uncontrollable. I would go home every day after school and tell my family how difficult these kids were. They don't listen, they don't care, and they need to change if we, as a community, are going to succeed. Later, when walking through the building, I saw those same "awful" kids sitting attentively, doing their work in another teacher's classroom. I realized then that the students weren't the problem; I was the problem. I had to change, and I did.

Adelaide Sanford, the most renowned educator in New York City and one of my mentors, was an elementary school principal located in the middle of a housing project in Brooklyn. Her school remains exemplary, with excellent instruction and stellar results. Ms. Sanford successfully surrounded her students with outstanding adults who genuinely cared about them. Just around the corner was another school that was failing miserably. Both schools served students from the same housing projects. Why does one school succeed while the other fails? What factors have changed? I asked this question during a presentation I gave to educators in Washington, D.C., and one participant responded, "You are telling us, 'It's the teachers, stupid!'" He was absolutely right.

The moment I walked into the building for my interview as a French teacher, I saw Kente cloth hanging from the ceilings and beautiful, student, Afrocentric artwork on the walls. A friendly woman security guard with a hearty laugh welcomed me at the door. I could immediately sense an aura of cultural pride and awareness, and I knew that this was the right place for me. I walked into the principal's office only to be met by a tall man with long salt-and-pepper dreads draping down his back—Principal Rock. I later met the assistant principal and was mesmerized by the naturally curly, silver hair in a long braid flowing down her back. I saw teachers with dreadlocks, twists, and fros. In a world where, as Black professionals, we feel forced to suppress how we were created to conform to what society says we should look like if we are to be leaders or teach other people's children, this was so refreshing. In this neighborhood between Bed-Stuy and Red Hook (pre-gentrification), it was so important for the children coming into that building to see examples of Black excellence and pride. I saw happy, confident students walking with purpose to their destinations, and I knew that I was home. Banneker taught its students to explore the world beyond their immediate environment. They were globally ready before it had become the new catchphrase. Students traveled to various continents and learned about world cultures. They expressed themselves in poetry, studied film, and took African dance classes and robotics. They excelled in STEM. Banneker had some of the best educators I have ever encountered in my twenty-one years of teaching. It was like a school from a TV show. And the teachers were students, too. We learned how to see the student as an individual and not take certain behaviors personally, but instead learn how to reach a child on a personal level, try to understand and help him grow, and achieve new personal goals. We learned how to look beyond just the subject that we teach, but to look at the role we play in preparing that child for the future from a much broader lens. The relationships and experiences I had at Banneker have shaped and molded me into the educator that I am today. I would not have changed a thing. —C. Toppin, Staff, 2008

HIGHLIGHTING TWO TEACHERS

In 2003, in New York State, so many students failed the end-of-year Physics Regents exams that the state had to invalidate the scores. Principals received a memo stating that the passing score would be drastically lowered so that more students could pass. When I heard this news, I rushed to speak with our physics teacher, Mr. Thompson, to find out how it would impact our passing rate. This was our first year taking the exam, so we only had one class. He said it wouldn't have changed for us because all our students passed the initial test! I couldn't believe it. How did that happen when students at some of the top schools in New York City failed at such a high rate? The answer was simple. We had a strong teacher who connected well with his students. He showed incredible dedication. His lessons were clear, and he spent hours working with his class after school. I am proud to say Mr. Thompson has become an exemplary school leader.

When principals have a tough day, many visit a special classroom to de-stress. My retreat room belonged to Ms. Fischer. She was small in stature yet had a powerful presence. She never yelled but could check you with one look if you got out of line. She was the best math teacher I've ever known. She could motivate students with her charisma, sense of humor, and dedication to young people. One year, she managed to get an entire class to pass two different math Regents exams in the same school year. This was unheard of.

She allowed her students to explore new and creative ideas. When you walked into her classroom, you saw a community of excited learners. Students worked well together and supported one another. It was beautiful to witness. Whatever drama I was experiencing before visiting her classroom no longer seemed important. Seeing Black children engaged and excited about learning warmed my heart. We were going to be okay. Ms. Fischer is a true hero.

She was able to create meaningful bonds in her classroom. The students felt loved there and looked forward to her presence. Her classes were packed after school and on Saturdays. I was surprised to see school troublemakers sitting in her classroom on Saturday afternoons. Students didn't have to be there, but they were getting what the early segregated students had: a safe, no-nonsense, inspiring space that felt like home—or at least what home should have felt like.

What made Banneker special for me? The answer to this question is unequivocally the teachers. The teachers didn't just teach their designated subject; they taught important life lessons and impacted my life in a way that I've never forgotten. Ms. Fischer could look at me and immediately see that I needed more than just a math lesson; she opened her doors to me and helped me believe in myself. I can say without hesitation that I would not have gone to college without her mentorship. —M. Vargas, Class of 2003

Principal's Office, Benjamin Banneker High School, Brooklyn, New York

October 30, 2000

Rock: Sit down, Coach.

Coach: Uh oh, Rock. This doesn't sound good. The security guard said to see you as soon as I came in. What's up?

Rock: His mother was here today. He is back.

Coach: Who is back?

Rock: Gary.

Coach: Back where?

Rock: Here, Coach. We got him a new schedule and everything. He is in class. His mother said he missed the school, and despite the advice of friends and family, she allowed him to return.

Coach: Unbelievable.

Rock: Believe it. Would he be eligible to play this year, Coach?

Coach: Yeah, but I need to think about team chemistry.

Rock: But Gary could help get us to The Garden. How does Clyde say it? "The World's Most Famous Arena."

Coach: Maybe we just let him start out playing JV. Our guys are doing great.

Rock: You're the boss, Coach. You won last night at Jefferson?

Coach: Yeah. We are 4-0.

Rock: Damn, Saunders, you guys are playing well. You have a scrappy team. I like how the guards are pressing all over the court. Will is showing a lot of leadership, and Andy is playing pretty well for a sophomore. Thought he wouldn't be ready.

Coach: I thought he would be more nervous

Rock: Also, that new kid looks strong.

Coach: He was having some trouble adjusting in school. A few teachers said he was coming late to class and not doing assignments. He's learning how we do things here. We had a conversation with him and his mom. He is making the necessary adjustments. Gotta remember, students weren't that focused at his other school.

Rock: Yeah, but he can't bring any nonsense here, Coach.

Coach: You sure Gary is back, Rock? I haven't heard anything.

Rock: Come on. Let's go upstairs. I'll take you to his class.

5

LEARNING THROUGH THE LENS OF BLACK CULTURE

Banneker felt like a big family. I especially appreciated that everything was taught through the lens of Black culture, which allowed us to be ourselves in a world that didn't accept us.

—J. Barnes, Class of 2007

Besides recruiting the best instructors, Benjamin Banneker Academy's other crucial educational approach was to recognize, embrace, and use cultural influences as instructional tools and resources. Since Banneker's enrollment was 96 percent Black and Latino, our students were encouraged to view their academic aspirations within the context of their ethnic heritage. They understood that racial pride, values, priorities, and perspectives enriched their learning. Therefore, they were given assignments that allowed them to explore and share different aspects and traditions unique to their cultures. Approximately 11 percent of the students were Latino, and in my final year, their graduation rate was 100 percent. We considered them part of the African diaspora. They also had a rich and unique culture and history, and we tried to honor their distinctive contributions to the school environment and our larger community through our programs and celebrations.

Teachers continually found ways to incorporate the Black experience into the educational curriculum. Our students went on many college tours, mainly to Historically Black Colleges and Universities. Ms. Jamison, one of our teachers, started a film festival where students made films celebrating their experiences. Some students worked on a revitalization plan for downtown Brooklyn. We offered clubs for students to explore, such as chess, poetry, acting, and dance.

We brought jazz musicians in to perform for the students in the cafeteria during lunch. They could continue eating, play chess or spades, or choose to sit at the front and listen to the musicians. I was surprised by how many students went up to speak with the jazz musicians. The kids were under no obligation to listen or talk with them, but we knew that early exposure to America's only original art form was important and enriching.

I often wish I had introduced a jazz program to the school and invited local musicians to teach jazz to interested students. It would have been a great opportunity for aspiring musicians to receive serious musical training in a Black environment where their culture was highly valued. Many talented Black students attend predominantly white performing arts high schools, and we could have provided them with a different option.

Banneker's mascot was an African warrior. One year, the NYC Department of Education wanted to remove all nick-names referencing warriors out of respect for Native Americans. We made it clear that we would not change our name because we are African warriors and proud of that part of our heritage. To us, this was a battle worth fighting.

Vanessa Walker describes this type of socialization as passing on cultural capital to students, a practice also prevalent in the early segregated Southern schools. She further emphasizes that good teaching can only happen with this personal and cultural understanding. Through classroom discussions, theatrical plays, group forums, and other special programs, students were encouraged to discuss what it's like being an African American or Latino student in America. Our kids took trips to New Orleans after Hurricane Katrina to support survivors. Ms. Terry Samuels, another one of our Banneker teachers, proposed the idea and accompanied the students to New Orleans, where they saw the storm's aftermath firsthand. On other trips, our students followed the Freedom Riders' historical trail through the South and took a tour re-creating the Underground Railroad to the North. This hands-on learning was actively promoted and carried out by our teachers with Banneker students.

> I was nominated by Mr. Rock to attend a civil rights tour among the Southern states. The queue was already filled, but I wanted to go so badly and expressed an interest in our history. Rock made it happen! Changed my entire perspective on life, my culture, and history!!! —K. Turner, Class of 2003

* * *

The most exciting and meaningful learning experiences for our students were the school trips and educational excursions outside the U.S. Our students traveled as far as Africa, accompanied by staff and parents. During these trips, they visited homes and schools where they observed evidence of self-respect and a strong work ethic among the African people.

Another teacher, Ms. K. Samuels, organized the African diaspora trips. She believed it was essential for students to experience the beauty of the African continent and its people firsthand. She worked hard organizing fundraisers, arranging travel itineraries, and ensuring that everyone had the required vaccinations. She held regular meetings with parents regarding all arrangements. Seeing Ms. Samuels engaged with students—planning, fundraising, and managing the many details of this international trip—was inspiring as I often visited her classroom after school. Most parents lacked the resources, so fundraising was necessary. Dances and bake sales were organized, and the school store became a valuable learning experience while raising the needed funds. Students learned how to work together toward an important goal. Ms. Samuels was a remarkable teacher. The idea and execution of this huge project came from her love and dedication to our students' educational growth and exposure. She worked tirelessly without extra pay to make multiple trips happen. Another teacher, Mr. Shabaka, assisted with the itinerary and logistics of the Senegal trip. He was a frequent traveler to Africa and arranged many of the cultural visits we made in Senegal, also serving as our guide. Both teachers demonstrated the same spirit and commitment found in the hearts of those early Black teachers.

On one international trip, I had to make two critical decisions as the school principal. The students and staff had saved all year for a trip to the West Coast of Africa. They sold candy, had bake sales, solicited donations, and raised over $30,000 for a trip to Senegal and The Gambia. One week before the trip, the new superintendent said she wouldn't sign off on the trip. She thought going out of the country was problematic and wasn't giving her permission for the students to go, even though New York City students had been traveling to Europe and other countries for years. The previous superintendent, Dr. Young, had always been supportive. Her decision posed a significant dilemma. If the students went on the trip and something happened, I'd be screwed. If they didn't go, their hard work would have been for nothing, and the students would miss out on a fantastic opportunity. As if that weren't enough, I also needed to decide if "Craig," a troubled student with a history of noncompliance, could go on the trip. He was suspended several times at his previous school and had failed most of his classes. What was I going to do with him?

I knew what I had to do. It was a gamble, but I couldn't let this superintendent disappoint all those students. We were going without her approval. As for Craig, I allowed him to come too. The kid was unpredictable and could go off anywhere at any time, but legally, I couldn't stop him. These were two potentially career-ending decisions, so I decided I needed to go and take that trip with our thirty students, five parents, and five teachers. I had planned to relax on a beach in Barbados during spring break, but I knew I had to go and make sure Craig didn't start an international incident. How would it look if something happened on the school trip while I was lounging on a beach, soaking up the sun?

Instead, on that crisp April morning, I woke up early and got on the bus parked in front of the school. Along with the students, teachers, and parents, we all made our way to John F. Kennedy Airport to begin our journey to Senegal. I smiled as the excited students boarded the plane. I gave Craig a look that said, *Yes, I am here and watching you, and I will not tolerate any foolishness.* However, I had to repeatedly scold him for acting up during the flight. A flight attendant also asked me to talk to him. Changing his seat and having him sit right next to me was the best solution I could think of in midair. This trip was going to be a lot of fun.

THEY WERE BLACK. ALL BLACK.

On the first night at the hotel in Senegal, I saw Craig running through the hallways, so I had to move him to a different room. I spoke sternly to him, but he didn't respond, which became an ongoing issue. Other teachers also complained about his behavior, and I thought about sending him home. However, it was only the first day, and someone would need to escort him back, which would mean missing out on the trip themselves.

On the second day, I stayed close to Craig as we interacted with the African people. He seemed more at ease talking to African students and felt the warmth and friendliness of the locals. That evening, I only had to reprimand him once.

The next day, I watched him closely as we took a long boat ride to the slave castles in Senegal. I didn't want him to push anyone overboard, so during the ride, I sat next to him, and we marveled at the sights and talked. When we reached the slave castles, the guide, noticing that we were all Black, told us to wait and said we'd get a special tour. About an hour later, we went inside, and I saw Craig walking solemnly with the other kids. Everyone was quiet as the guide explained what happened inside those walls. There was no playing around.

While the students sat in the small room with the *Door of No Return,* I searched for Craig. He was quiet, and I could see tears in his eyes. He started sobbing, as did some of the other students. One of the teachers put her arm around him. It was a moving experience for all of us—a feeling only those who experienced it could truly understand.

After exploring the castles, we returned for lunch, and Craig sat with the other students, chatting and joking around. He looked relaxed and was clearly having fun with them. I didn't walk with him for the rest of the day. I marveled at this change, as did the other adults. We all scratched our heads, wondering if this was the same young man.

Over the next seven days, I didn't feel the need to walk alongside Craig because he was able to manage his behavior. We had no issues in the rooms at night. I enjoyed spending time with him and all the other students for the rest of our trip in Africa.

We visited schools and experienced a memorable musical tribute at one of the rural compounds. The Africans made us feel completely at home, and despite their limited resources, they shared everything with us. The natural dignity and pride of the African people rubbed off on the students. The young people we met were fun-loving and kind to one another. There was no insulting each other in jest, as our kids sometimes do. They were very respectful to their teachers. I was surprised when Craig sought me out to walk with him during several of the remaining tours.

Although the logistics for this trip were excellent, we experienced a frightening mishap. About eight of us missed the flight from Senegal to The Gambia because of a taxi breakdown. Instead, we had to take a long bus ride and a ferry. Fortunately, it was only the parents, one teacher, and me. Thank goodness, no students. The bus ride was over lengthy dirt roads, and the military stopped our van a couple of times, with machine guns slung across their bodies. They wanted to see our passports. It was all very nerve-wracking, but we made it to the ferry, took a long, crowded, bouncy ride to The Gambia, and met up with the rest of our group.

Ultimately, we arrived safely back in New York City, and I let out a huge sigh of relief. We made it home without any major drama. I greeted Craig's mother at the airport, hugged her, and told her I was so happy he had come along. She thanked me for giving her son this opportunity. Craig shook my hand and sincerely said, "Thanks." It would have been a real shame if I hadn't allowed this trip to happen. Everyone, both adults and students, had a transformative experience.

Craig is a different person now. So am I. The whole trip was touching. I felt a special connection with everyone who went on that journey. Seeing our homeland for the first time with the Banneker group is burned into my memory. None of this would have been possible without that special teacher, Ms. Karlene Samuels.

Banneker was an institution of excellence. The education, support, and love I received at Banneker shaped the woman I am today. I was able to sit in rooms with master educators, and they poured into me. They were invested in my development as a brilliant Black student. There was no other school that could've molded me the way Banneker did. I was able to see myself in the curriculum and in the choices the administration made on my behalf. I have lifelong relationships with my peers and some of the dynamic teachers from Banneker. I wish every child, especially of color, could have been fortunate to have the education and experience I had at Banneker! I'm a proud Warrior for life! I loved the school so much that I returned for a while as a substitute teacher! Special shoutout to Ms. Karlene Samuels, the African Tours, and the Class of 2005. —A. McNeill Class of 2005

Principal's Office, Benjamin Banneker High School, Brooklyn, New York

December 12, 2000

Rock: How is Gary doing, Coach?

Coach: He is coming to practice, but no games yet. Walking around like he is Kobe Bryant. The crew says he needs to be more humble, but the boy can play.

Rock: Don't take it out on him, Coach, because he left. He had a lot of outside forces steering him in that direction. He is a great kid. He kinda felt like he left his family when he transferred. He told me the love wasn't the same over there. Black love is strong.

Coach: Can't deny Gary has the skills. But Rock, I like these young kids we have playing. Nana is really playing well, too. He hangs out with a lot of tough kids but hasn't really had any problems here. I know if a fight broke out, I would want him on my side.

Rock: Damn, you guys haven't lost a game yet?

Coach: Yeah, our division is pretty weak. We're gonna have some trouble when we play the Manhattan and Bronx teams. Rock, were those our students on horseback riding up and down the street?

Rock: One of our parents, Wayne Powell, hooked it up. Now we have an Equestrian Club.

Coach: Damn, how many clubs have we got?

Rock: Yeah, it's a lot. Getting ready for the trip to Florida?

Coach: Everything is straight with the hotel and the Christmas tournament down there. Kids raised most of the money. Most of the teams are white—only two Black teams. Getting out of town will be a good experience for our kids. Most have never been on a plane.

6

ALL HANDS ON DECK

Banneker was special for me because it really gave me a sense of unity and pride. I didn't get to go to an HBCU, but I still feel like I got part of that experience being in Banneker.

—V. Fontus, Class of 2009

For me, Banneker was the manifestation of *The Village* that it took to raise a child. It was being proud to be Black without knowing that there was any other alternative to that sense of pride. It was reclaiming my family's Caribbean culture and OWNING it. It was being taught by teachers who looked like me... then finding out in my adulthood just how lucky I was to have had those experiences. Banneker was Black History every day. Banneker is home.

—S. Cutkelvin, Class 2003

A 1994 editorial in Newsweek magazine described a segregated school in the South as "a place where students never got the message that they were second-rate, unequal, unwanted… They did not see themselves as powerless victims because the teacher drilled into them that it was possible to overcome, but it took preparation. We wanted to be the best."[16] We adopted that approach at Banneker and emphasized to our students and the school community that effort and preparation lead to success. We were an effort-based school that shared many of the tenets proposed by University of Pittsburgh professor Lauren Resnick, who argues that an effort-based school replaces the idea that aptitude solely determines what and how much students learn with the belief that sustained and focused effort can produce high achievement for all students. Everything we did was designed to foster and support this effort. High minimum standards were set, and the curriculum was crafted to meet these standards. Resnick also said, "Some students will need extra time and expert instruction to meet these expectations. Providing that time and expertise helps send the message that effort is expected and that tough problems yield to sustained work."[17]

Banneker provided an intensive after-school program and tutoring on Saturdays to support students struggling academically. We insisted that these students participate in our tutoring programs. At first, most students protested and resisted, but we involved parents to encourage participation, and eventually, it became standard. Parent involvement is crucial to ensuring students attend extra classes and the programs our school partners set up. These extras make all the difference.

Students in our Saturday program received phone calls if they were late. We specifically hired someone whose only job was to make those calls because we knew how important it was to get parental support. We held students and parents accountable, and parents almost always came through. It's a myth that Black parents do not support their children in school. They may not be able to attend all the parent meetings, but when we made it clear that we were offering extra help and needed their support, they responded. We wanted their children to develop a strong work ethic, and these parents responded just as parents and caretakers did in the historically segregated schools in the South. We encouraged our students, and parents supported our efforts.

During our tutoring sessions, students worked in groups and dedicated three to four hours to focused work. On any given Saturday, about one-third of the student body might be at school, making it feel like a typical school day. It was crucial for students to recognize and understand the link between effort and success. *Once young people realize they can control their academic success through hard work, nothing will hold them back!*

I advise principals to establish comprehensive after-school programs if they want to transform a school. They can't replace ineffective teachers immediately. One hour a day of focused, clear tutoring with a strong educator can make up for five days of inadequate instruction. We had several part-ners who worked with our students after school. One was the Institute for Student Achievement (ISA), and another was the Banneker Community Development Corporation (CDC). Both had offices in the basement of our building, and their teachers built strong relationships with our students. One of our graduates even named his art gallery after a teacher, Mr. Bishop. Partners can be challenging to manage, but if you find the right ones, they can bring effective teachers and counsel-ors into the school. The CDC and ISA staff understood our vision and provided the support needed for our success. Dr. Laprade, the director of the CDC, and Mr. Lippold, ISA's director, along with their staff, made a significant difference in our children's lives.

One positive outcome of schooling during the pandemic was the use of virtual classrooms. If I were a principal today, my strongest teachers would work online with small groups of students after school and on Saturdays. I worked with several schools during the pandemic where administrators removed distracted students from the classroom and placed them in a virtual room with a strong teacher. The students followed the classroom teacher online, stayed focused, and did not disrupt the class.

In 2004, Banneker launched a program in partnership with Viola Abbott, an outstanding elementary school principal, where high school students tutored elementary and middle school students. The results were remarkable. Many middle school students in this program passed a Math Regents exam *before* entering high school. This program was established before New York City middle schools introduced an Algebra Regents program. Our initiative brought several added benefits: middle school teachers learned the high school math curriculum from our teachers, many high school students who tutored went on to pursue careers in teaching, and middle schoolers were excited about attending high school because their tutors served as role models.

One year, we had two aspiring principals who interned at our school. They had to report their work hours to the Department of Education to receive their stipends. I received a call from the New York City DOE Investigators' office questioning whether the interns were at our school at 11:00 p.m. on one occasion and midnight on another. The caller didn't believe those late hours and stated that no previously submitted timesheets showed similar times. He suspected fraud was occurring. I told the investigator that the interns were there, along with our other staff, working on ways to improve the school for our children. We valued work-life balance, so these late hours weren't common. However, our teachers were dedicated and ready to step up whenever needed, and we appreciated that.

In addition to the after-school and Saturday programs, we held an intensive all-day event called the Nine-to-Nine Program. The program took place three or four Saturdays before the State Regents Examinations. George Leonard, who taught biology, founded and ran the program. He was one of our twenty male educators. Students stayed at school for twelve hours in a single day, with breaks for lunch and dinner prepared by parents. This rigorous study program aimed to help students catch up on missed or incomplete work and prepare for exams. It also fostered a sense of accomplishment through sustained effort. Imagine staying in school from 9:00 a.m. to 9:00 p.m. It sounds exhausting, but students learned the value of maximum effort, which will benefit them later. Students received T-shirts that read, "I survived the nine to nine." Once again, a dedicated educator proposed a project to support our students, and we backed it wholeheartedly, reaping amazing results.

Due to the unique learning environment at Banneker Academy, our students visited and eventually attended some of the finest HBCUs in the country. Many of our male graduates gained acceptance to Morehouse College, the nation's top historically Black college for African American men. Many of our female students were admitted to Spelman College, the nation's leading historically Black college for African American women. These prestigious universities in Atlanta, Georgia, grew out of the South's historically segregated school system. Both institutions have produced some of America's most outstanding Black leaders. Dr. Martin Luther King Jr., Senator Raphael Warnock, and filmmaker Spike Lee are all alumni of Morehouse. Child advocate Marian Wright Edelman, politician Stacey Abrams, and renowned author Alice Walker are among Spelman's notable graduates. Banneker students pursued higher education at these historic colleges and universities, demonstrating that our teaching philosophies and educational commitment helped students see the value of attending Black institutions.

Benjamin Banneker was probably the only school in all of Brooklyn that gave high school students a taste of an HBCU and an Ivy League institution all at once. The school spirit was unmatched, and the Black representation in staff and leadership embodied the essence of the Black college experience. There were Black people in STEM standing in front of Black and Brown children. There were Black people who taught us history in a way that was authentic to the Black experience and not just what the curriculum told them to teach. —D. Robinson, Class of 2007

Banneker was super pro-Black. I wouldn't have had it any other way. Everyone exemplified Black Pride—from the afros to the locs! We learned the truth about this nation called America. I'd never forget my first week of class during freshman year. A teacher started class by saying, "Christopher Columbus was an idiot." LOL. That stuck with me. —B. Boure, Class of 2008

Principal's Office, Benjamin Banneker High School, Brooklyn, New York

December 24, 2000

Rock: What do you mean the plane tickets to Florida didn't go through?

Coach: Some kind of glitch with the airlines. A storm is coming, and they can't guarantee our round trip, plus the hotel won't give us a refund.

Rock: What about getting the money back from the airline, Saunders? That's thousands of dollars.

Coach: They said the check is coming but won't be here for a few days. This is also gonna mess up their tournament down South if teams can't get there. I don't think there's anything we can do.

Rock: Kids are really disappointed?

Coach: Yeah, Rock. Maybe we can take a bus.

Rock: Coach, be realistic. How are you gonna take a bus all the way from New York to Florida? The kids will be exhausted. That's twenty hours. Where would you get a bus at the last minute? Plus, you'd have to pay for two drivers and put them up in the hotel.

Coach: We need to do something, Rock.

Rock: We have a contract with one bus company, but how will we get a purchase order on Christmas Eve, and what drivers want to drive on Christmas?

Coach: Come on, Rock. The kids want to go.

Rock: Let me call Mr. P to see how best to get a purchase order. Hope he is home. Was Gary going?

Coach: No, his mom won't let him. He hasn't been doing his chores, so he is staying home. Going on this trip is a good time for the team to bond. We need to discuss how best to fit Gary into our system.

Rock: Damn, Coach—Christmas Eve?

7

HOW WE TREAT ONE ANOTHER

As a substitute teacher early in my teaching career, Banneker set the bar for my expectations for other schools throughout the city, where I would eventually work. Sadly, so many of them didn't measure up. I was impressed by Banneker's unapologetic, affirming focus on Black people from the moment you entered the building. The walls were plastered with posters and murals. There were carvings and creative signage throughout the school. Teachers exemplified culture and style along with a staunch commitment to helping kids learn. It was a phenomenal experience to witness such Black positivity and excellence up close. I took it all with me.

—M. Fingal, Staff

School culture and climate are essential parts of a school building. When they are established properly, a school can become an exceptional place. If not, the atmosphere can be quite bleak. Outsiders quickly notice the culture as soon as they walk in. Visitors—whether parents, new students, or community members—observe how staff and students interact. Do people yell at each other, or do they speak kindly? Are people smiling, and what kind of language are they using? Visitors pick up on this instantly as they enter the building.

It's similar to what happens in a classroom. When a teacher establishes a strong classroom culture, new students quickly adapt. I have always been amazed that when a teacher was absent, students managed fine with a substitute if the teacher had set clear norms. It was almost as if the physical space reminded everyone how to behave. Most teachers understand that once a classroom culture—whether positive or negative—is in place, it's difficult to change.

The question then becomes: how do you establish such a culture in a school? Again, it's the people you bring into the building. You can't train people to smile and greet others genuinely. That would have to be part of their makeup. Some people are unhappy for no apparent reason. If they are in a school, they can spread that misery. We hired people with pleasant attitudes and who seemed genuinely happy. I've found that people with a certain Black consciousness, raised to respect themselves, tend to treat others that way.

When you entered our school, a friendly, engaging security guard greeted you in a well-lit foyer. Your first interaction at the school should feel warm and inviting. When you arrived at the office, a pleasant receptionist made it clear she was there to help in any way she could. If students were in the office, they would greet visitors, letting them know the environment was family-friendly. Students moved freely in and out of the main office and my office. My door was always open unless I was in a meeting.

While students walked to and from class inside the build-ing, they talked and enjoyed each other's company. Security personnel and teachers sometimes had to move them along, but their interactions were firm and respectful, not aggressive or demeaning. We occasionally had fights or confrontations, but they were rare. When people from the Department of Education visited and praised the students' good behavior, I wasn't sure how to respond. I was glad they recognized our kids were respectful and well-behaved, but why are people surprised when Black kids behave properly? We set high standards, and our students met them. That was normal for us.

Not only was there a sense of peacefulness at Banneker, but it was also clear that this was a Black space. One year, the district sent a Black social worker to our school to work with some of our kids. After thirty minutes, she left. When I spoke to her supervisor later that day, I asked why she had left so quickly. He told me she preferred to take a position elsewhere because our school was too Afrocentric. I had to laugh. That's the vibe we were giving off, and if you couldn't roll with that, then see ya!

Sometimes, a white family would visit the school as a potential place for one of their children. They heard about our test scores and course offerings, and since we were in a gentrifying neighborhood, we showed them around. They would be impressed by the classes, but almost none would actually enroll. We were friendly and welcoming, yet unapologetically Black. All our decision-makers were people of color. The leaders, teachers, students, and parents were Black. All Black. That was too much for some white folks—and for some Black people, too.

On the other hand, we had Black parents who wanted their children to attend a school like ours. Repeatedly, I heard comments like, "I want my son to be around strong Black men who will look out for him." We welcomed everyone, and the few white or Asian students we had received the same care as the Black kids. We embraced students of all races and cultures but celebrated our Blackness without needing outside validation.

We would have visits from the district promoting the latest pedagogy. We accepted some, but many we didn't. We knew what our children needed, and the leadership downtown realized this, so after a while, they left us alone. They knew the community was behind us, and we initially had a strong superintendent in Dr. Young, who supported and protected us from harassment.

Community support is essential, and I now recommend that new principals work to earn the trust of their stakeholders. You will need their support because Black achievement, rooted in a strong Black culture without external input, might be perceived as threatening. Critics will find many reasons to criticize the school, even if it has high scores, satisfied students and teachers, and an overall positive learning environment. Given the many challenges schools face, missed deadlines or uncontrollable incidents are sometimes used to damage the school's reputation.

I wasn't an in-your-face defender like my mentor and friend, Principal Frank Mickens, from the well-known Brooklyn Boys and Girls High School, but the Department of Education knew that if they approached me the wrong way, there would be trouble. Preserving your dignity is more important than almost anything else. I never looked for a fight, but I wouldn't tolerate disrespect. Being assertive without being aggressive is a delicate balancing act that all leaders must manage. You can't let anyone take away your joy or love for your profession and the people you care about. Respect is crucial, but don't feel you have to prove your worth every day. You are already deserving.

Countless others and I are the humans we are because of the love and knowledge we received at Banneker. Currently, I teach at our sister school, Bedford Academy; I am in awe at how much, almost twenty years later, this place significantly affected me as a Black person, woman, intellectual, revolutionary, and educator. Banneker was a learning oasis of Black excellence, smack dab in the middle of Brooklyn, and a spark to my metamorphosis, creating who I am and who I strive to be. Banneker is family!
—C. Anderson, Class of 2006

THEY WERE BLACK. ALL BLACK.

Principal's Office, Benjamin Banneker High School, Brooklyn, New York

January 3, 2001

Rock: How did it go, Coach?

Coach: Trip was fine. We left before the last game. Bus driver wanted to get back because the blizzard was coming. That was a long bus ride.

Rock: I saw the article in the paper about "Kids' Florida Trip Saved." The reporter called me. Said it would be a good Christmas story.

Coach: I tell you, Rock, there is one thing I will never do again in my life if I live to be one hundred years old. I will never ever go on a bus ride for twenty hours with twenty teenagers—so much silliness.

Rock: Glad you made it back safely. The kids told me they had a good time. I saw Gary playing in the JV game yesterday. It wasn't fair. He was killing those kids. Must have been ten out of eleven from the field.

Coach: Yeah, Rock, he has really developed. He's humbled a little, too. Meshing well with the guys in practice. Seems happy in the school. Doing well in his classes and spends a lot of time talking with teachers after school. He is well-liked by almost everyone. Unusual for a young phenom.

Rock: You gotta like the young man. He is a pleasure to be around.

Coach: We are winning without him, but I'm just not sure how far we can go in the playoffs if he doesn't play. Chemistry is good. For now, we will let him play JV and practice with us. The other coaches still feel a little resentment that he left us. Some feel he can sit out this year and play the next two years.

Rock: How do you feel about that, Coach?

Coach: He is a kid, and children make mistakes and need to be forgiven, but at the same time, it's important to remember that there are consequences for your decisions. I'm conflicted, and then there is MSG. What a thrill that would be for all the guys and the school.

Rock: Do what you think is best for the kids, Coach.

Coach: You were at the game yesterday?

Rock: Yeah, it was a good, strong win. I wanted to visit that school. I was the Assistant Principal there. A funny thing happened when I was standing outside the building. The school's principal heard that Banneker's principal was outside, so she sent a teacher outside to ask the principal to come into her office. I was standing outside talking with our athletic director. Here I was in a suit and tie with our white AD, who was wearing a sweat suit, and the teacher went right up to him and said, "Excuse me, sir, our principal wants to see you."

Coach: Hate to laugh, but that's messed up, Rock.

Rock: Black man with locs can't be a principal? The AD is one of only two white staff members in the whole school, and she picks him.

Coach: You checked out any of the girls' games, Rock? They look good.

Rock: The girls' team is playing well. I went to see them play a couple of times. They press just like you guys. They say I treat them like second-class citizens, so I must go to more games. I can't believe how much the girls' game has changed in the past ten years.

Coach: They are good. I might coach girls one day. They seem more receptive to coaching.

Rock: Their coach has them playing hard. A couple of kids may get scholarships. Actually, I think two of their players are better than some of your guys.

Coach: Don't say that, Rock. But one day, the girls were scrimmaging the guys, and Latoya crossed up one of our guys and laid him up. The whole gym broke out laughing. He was embarrassed but took it like a man and laughed it off. Thought I might have to talk him off the ledge, but he was cool.

Rock: He learned a lesson. Don't sleep on the females. They can play.

8

THE KINSHIP ASSOCIATION

I'm GRATEFUL for attending Benjamin Banneker Academy for Community Development! That name was so FITTING! God really had his hand in that academic setting! It was the extended family and home I never knew I needed. Once a Warrior, always a Warrior. Teachers, administrators, counselors, and supporting staff felt like aunts and uncles. They supported and nurtured every dream and talent. There was literally nothing unattainable. The strength of the school was its culture. The belief in achievement for all was ingrained in every lesson taught, whether it was echoed in a classroom or passing in the hallway. Schools are known to have PTA meetings, but we had Kinship meetings. Teachers organized clubs tailored to uplifting students, paired with the responsibility of knowing our true history. I am an educator and in the beginning stages of starting a school with my brother. Many of my non-negotiables came from my experiences while attending Banneker. I know we have a lot of work ahead, but I know that I have a phenomenal blueprint. Banneker equipped its students to dismiss all things doubtful and bask in the light of endless possibilities. Banneker, I thank you!

—Z. McCoy, Class of 2009

In the education field, we often hear that Black parents are not involved in their children's schooling. They don't attend PTA meetings, check homework, or take school seriously. Despite these assertions, in my forty years of experience in education, I have never met a parent who didn't want their child to succeed academically. Many parents may not have had good relationships with schools and teachers in the past, which might make them skeptical of their child's school.

When I started teaching, I would visit the homes of students who were difficult to manage. Surprisingly, I never received a negative response from the parents. They always welcomed me into their homes. It became clear that some parents were dealing with a lot and couldn't participate in school activities. As educators, we work for the parents, and they trust us with their most valued possessions—their children. We have students for about six or seven hours each day, and we must ensure they are safe, challenged, and treated fairly, whether the parents are involved or not. We all know that parental participation greatly influences student academic progress, but if life circumstances make it hard or impossible for parents to get involved, so be it. Their children still need to be educated.

I disagree with some educators about the importance of parent involvement. Naturally, parents should participate in school activities as much as possible. We should reach out and invite them to all essential school meetings, parent-teacher conferences, and other relevant events. However, *the lack of parental involvement shouldn't be an excuse for failure*. Getting adults more involved as parents can be a very difficult task for educators. Schools can try to change an adult's mindset, but this may take time and resources that many schools simply don't have. We can't spend too much time trying to change grown-ups. I believe we have a much better chance of changing a fourteen-year-old's mindset, given that they are in school with us and we have their attention for many hours each day.

When I arrived at Banneker, some parents appeared confrontational. They wanted the best for their children, and so did I. It took time to get on the same page and build a strong relationship. Parents mainly want to be heard, and their requests can be met with a little effort. They want to know that their kids will be safe and that the building maintains a sense of order.

The parents and community members saw me at the corner of Myrtle Avenue every school day as their children went home. I made sure to have three or four adults present at the corner each afternoon after school. The school safety officers initially hesitated about going to the corner, but those who connected with our kids and embraced our school philosophy went willingly. The students left the school to go home, walking down one long block and then taking public buses, walking to the train station, or walking to the housing projects four blocks away.

While we were there, we didn't tolerate any nonsense. Sometimes, kids enjoy fighting and watching fights. Many times, teen outsiders would come and confront our students after school. Our presence prevented most trouble; the community and parents understood and respected that.

I scheduled no meetings during dismissal, and it would have to be a serious emergency for me not to be on the corner.

Sometimes, if a parent or a Department of Education official wanted to speak to me, they knew they could find me there after school. I often remind new principals of how important dismissal is and encourage them to be outside during that time. When parents are looking for a school for their children, I tell them to visit during dismissal and observe what's happening. Are students leaving in an organized manner, and are there adults present to ensure their safety? To assess a school's level of organization, visit when students are leaving for the day.

We had a core group of parents we could always rely on. They attended Kinship meetings, which other schools call Parent-Teacher Association (PTA) meetings, and these parents also served on the leadership teams. Whenever we needed volunteers, I knew they would step up. They chaperoned school dances and proms and went on trips with the students. They organized fundraisers, managed the school store, and took part in book clubs and holiday gatherings. We also held workshops on effective parenting that many found helpful. Sometimes parents paid for teachers' dinners during Open School nights. Overall, parents played a vital role in our school's success.

In the early segregated schools, Black parents played an essential role in supporting the school. They sacrificed a lot, just like Banneker's parents did, because we were all part of the same community. I grew close to these parents; the kinship was sincere.

When there were academic or disciplinary issues, our counselors or deans usually summoned parents. Parents would meet with school staff to resolve any issues. High school students face all kinds of personal challenges: peer pressure, family issues, sexual development, financial struggles, and natural growing pains. Often, students need to know there is an adult in the building they can trust and talk to, someone who will listen. Parents value that there are adults who can connect with their children in meaningful and necessary ways.

Our guidance counselors handled most of the heavy lifting, but teachers and administrators all mentored students and helped them succeed. I didn't have to teach the educators how to interact with Black parents; they instinctively knew how.

A school's graduation rate is high when students facing difficulties have an adult in the building they can connect with. If a student was absent for a few days, a call would be made to their home to check if everything was okay. It wasn't so much "we gotcha," but more "let's work this out together. I need you to be successful. I am on your side." All kids need encouragement, support, and validation. Our staff would be there if parents couldn't fully provide this level of support. Teenagers and parents sometimes butt heads, and I believe parents appreciate having another voice they can count on to help guide their child. When parents see that you respect their children and treat them with dignity, they will not view the school as an adversary but as another part of the extended family, capable of helping.

> I had an awesome experience attending Banneker. The atmosphere was just incredible. We were more than just students and staff; we were a family. The teachers really cared about us and our futures and made sure we were prepared for the real world. We had a lot of cool teachers who taught us a lot but were also down-to-earth. We could talk to them about anything and didn't have to worry about being judged or being turned away. If we had a problem, they tried their best to help us. I loved attending Banneker and being a part of the Banneker family.
> —J. Murray, Class of 2003

Principal's Office, Benjamin Banneker High School, Brooklyn, New York

February 22, 2001

Coach: Sad day yesterday, Rock

Rock: Yeah, saw your guys at the funeral for Jamal.

Coach: When I saw him in the hallways, he was always smiling. Though he didn't play sports, a lot of the guys on the team were close to him.

Rock: Yeah, Coach. He was a wonderful kid. Good student. Hard worker. Tragic. Hard to resolve in my mind. He wasn't the intended target—wrong party, wrong time. Shot dead. Unbelievable. Another Black boy gunned down. His family is devastated. The school is devastated. Did you see the memorial in the front?

Coach: Yeah. When does the violence and senseless killing end?

Rock: You let your daughter go to these parties, Coach?

Coach: Absolutely not, but I can't keep her locked up forever. I don't even know if we should play our game tomorrow.

Rock: Up to you, Coach. I would understand either way you go. Want me to talk to the guys? You can bring them in. I know they are hurting.

9

HOW WE RAISE OUR CHILDREN

Banneker was excellence on another level. We were talented and intelligent, yet we had the propensity to be some "bad behind" teenagers. Nevertheless, everyone seemed to have a vision for themselves, regardless of life circumstances. Our teachers looked like us; they were smart, hip, and fashionably astute. The teachers of Banneker actively engaged in molding our character, challenging us to become the greatness we were destined to be. As a Banneker Alumna, you can still see our resilience to rise above and beyond any occasion in our professions, how we raise our children, and in our expectations from the communities we reside in.

—A. White, Class of 2007

The first thing you notice when visiting a failing school is that many classrooms are chaotic and disorganized. The students are not paying attention, and too many are disrespecting the adults and each other. They are using foul language and speaking to each other aggressively. The adults are yelling threats, and there is a sense of vulnerability and unease. Kids cannot learn in an environment where it's a free-for-all and mutual respect hasn't been established.

So, how do you keep order? That's a challenge facing schools across the nation.

Rules must be clearly outlined, and enforcement must be consistent. The issues mostly involve a small group of teachers, but what if that group received better training to manage disciplinary problems? Or what if they left the school altogether and were replaced by more effective teachers? The impact could be significant! Nearly every principal will tell you that most student disciplinary issues stem from a small fraction of the staff.[18]

Instructional skills can be learned, but developing a strong presence in front of a classroom may come from an innate or instinctive ability. A positive classroom environment is not determined by a teacher's stature, gender, or race; however, teachers who want to be successful with their students need to maintain control of the classroom. It might take new teachers a few years to build a confident and commanding presence. However, all teachers must project this when teaching students of color. *"I am in charge, and I need you to follow the rules so you can learn"* must be communicated clearly through demeanor and attitude—similar to the expectations set by teachers in early segregated schools.

Banneker had a peaceful atmosphere with a firm undertone. The students knew the adults were in charge, but our school didn't have a prison-like mindset or environment. When students walked the halls, they didn't have to walk single file with their eyes straight ahead, as I have seen in some schools. The expectation was that students would behave; if they didn't, they would be called out. We understood that children could sometimes get out of hand, but their behavior rarely warranted extreme punishment.

Generally, the teachers at Banneker managed their students' behavioral issues on their own, and when they couldn't, the administration stepped in. We seldom suspended students. In serious cases, we asked parents to keep the child at home until the problem was resolved.

We resolved most issues by meeting with the kids who were experiencing problems. We used conflict-resolution techniques and reminded students how we are all connected. Our ancestors might have been on the same slave ship, and we are linked through generations and need to respect that legacy. There was no reason to fight your family members. Through ongoing dialogue, we effectively reached most kids and only had a few severe incidents.

We didn't tolerate gang activity or outsiders harassing our students. Despite our best efforts, the drama happening in the community sometimes spilled into the school. During my ten years at Banneker, we lost several students to gun violence. It was painful and frustrating because we couldn't control what happened outside the school.

New York City principals in schools of color spend too much time dealing with the police. Many of our students are victims of youth violence, and sometimes, the police need to be called to keep them safe. There have been cases where our kids fell victim to sexual predators. Other times, the police accused our students of criminal behavior. Students often felt the police were unfair and looked to adults to advocate for them. The local police knew me well as someone who would fight for our kids.

A friend of mine, who was a police captain, told me a story she heard at a meeting of New York City police brass. Police leaders were preparing a new commander who had recently taken over our school's police precinct. The new commander asked the outgoing commander, "What's up with this guy, Rock? He is asking for a lot."

The senior commander responded, "Deal with him—he is not going away. He is not going away!" Hearing this story made me feel good because I wanted the community to know that I was not going away when it came to supporting our children.

For a few years, we had an officer assigned to our school who served as a liaison between the school and the police. He knew our students, and there was mutual respect. He did an excellent job.

There were a few instances in which a student was arrested, but we did not allow the arrest to occur on school property. We already have too many images of Black people being paraded in handcuffs seared into young minds, and we weren't going to let Banneker play any role in reinforcing those stereotypes. The student would come outside with an administrator and then be escorted to the precinct. Students were not handcuffed inside the building, escorted down hallways, and led to a waiting police vehicle as seen in other schools.

I remember two times when the police arrested our students for assaulting an officer. One incident happened at a train station, where a young man was accused of jumping the turnstile. There was pushing and shoving, and an officer was hurt. Prosecutors wouldn't offer this student a plea deal because an officer was injured. The young man had never been in trouble before, and with a good attorney, he successfully demonstrated that the altercation was not his fault. He was found not guilty.

Another incident involved a young woman witnessing a fight between other students in her neighborhood. She was not part of the fight herself. The police grabbed her, there was a struggle, and a police officer's jaw was broken. She was about five feet four, and the officers were all large men. The young woman refused to accept a plea deal, despite advice from others, including her mother and her pastor. When I spoke to her, she insisted she would not plead guilty to something she didn't do. She had never been in trouble before, but she could face years in prison if found guilty. I felt frightened for her, but I was also proud that she was standing her ground against powerful forces. She was eventually found not guilty, graduated from Banneker, and later from college.

I remember an honor student who was summoned to court because she used her train pass on a Saturday to get extra help with calculus. Passes are only valid on school days; Saturday isn't considered a school day. The police officer knew she was going to school; she had her books with her. Still, she received a summons to appear in court. Her grandmother was terrified for her. Even the judge rolled his eyes when we went to court. It was preposterous.

When I spoke with officers of color about these three incidents, they all agreed they would have handled things differently. There would not have been any court proceedings for any of these students. Sadly, it seemed the arresting officers saw our students as criminals rather than family members, as we did.

We accompanied our students to court whenever they were accused of a crime. I was called to testify many times before family court judges. If you've ever been to family court in Brooklyn, you know the despair on the faces in the waiting room. Sit there for a few hours and observe the families of color waiting for their cases to be heard. You see parents sitting next to young people, waiting for their futures decided by judges who hold their fates with their sentencing. It hurts to see beautiful Black and Brown children—some innocent, some not—faced with the heavy hand of the criminal justice system. I felt sympathy for the parents who wanted the best for their children but found themselves in this perilous situation.

The pull of street culture—gang activity, gun violence, and fast cash from illicit means—is powerful, and some of our students were pulled into criminal activities. We failed a few of them in this regard, which still saddens me. These are some of the daily pressures of adolescence in inner-city life. In the same way, the culture in our school building embraced and positively directed our students; the street culture also had an allure, but in a different direction. Young people are sometimes forced into gang activities in order to survive and cope with rivals. The pull of the streets must be countered by strong individuals who care about our children.

Allowing street violence to go unchallenged is the true crime, more than the actions of some of our children. Providing safe spaces for young people in urban settings has not been a high priority, and until that changes, even schools like Banneker will sometimes lose the tug-of-war to the streets.

Principal's Office, Benjamin Banneker High School, Brooklyn, New York

February 27, 2001

Rock: What the heck happened, Coach?

Coach: I forgot we had a game.

Rock: There goes our perfect record.

Coach: Damn, Rock, I feel terrible. They have the new online scheduling method, and I was confused by it.

Rock: I got a call from the commissioner looking for you yesterday.

Coach: We were practicing and getting ready for the playoffs. I feel so bad.

Rock: Don't stress it, Saunders. We are human, and we mess up sometimes.

Coach: You're not gonna fire me, are you?

Rock: No, Coach, but I might have to reconsider if you don't win this first playoff game. I'm just playing around. Winning or losing in the long run is not that important, but it does seem so in the short term. When I was a coach, I put so much emphasis on winning. Are we doing the kids a disservice by trying to get them to win so badly?

Coach: Playing hard and striving for excellence is what we want our kids to do. But something happens when the game starts. It becomes like life or death for the guys and me. After the game, I am good, but during the game, I want to destroy the other team. Why do we need to win so badly?

Rock: I think kids learn more from losing than winning. Anybody can win, but handling losing builds character. Much of life will be dealing with challenges, and our kids need to learn how to handle adversity and failure.

Coach: Martin Luther King said something like that. "The measure of a man is not where he stands when winning, but where he stands at times of challenge and failure."

Rock: Yeah, Coach, something like that. Our kids need help and guidance when facing trying circumstances. Too many get caught up in the criminal justice system because they didn't have the necessary decision-making tools to handle tough challenges.

Coach: You think they could have avoided it if they had played ball?

Rock: If they were surrounded by strong Black men like the crew you have, Saunders.

Coach: That's why we put that crew together. The kids interact with positive brothers with a common goal. We spend more time with the guys than their fathers, even if the dads are in the home. At practice every day and on Saturday, we are in their ears—constantly talking about right and wrong, decision-making, dealing with teachers, girlfriends, and parents. We become their other family. They form bonds they will never forget.

Rock: That's true, Coach. Unfortunately, this will probably be the end of organized basketball for most of our kids, but as you say, they are getting crucial life lessons.

Coach: Probably none of these kids will play ball in a D-1 college or the pros, except maybe Gary.

Rock: Just think what it would mean for them to play a game in MSG. They will remember that for the rest of their lives, Coach.

Coach: Rock, did you think you would one day play in the pros as a kid?

Rock: Yeah! I still do.

Coach: Now that's a good one.

10

THE DEPARTMENT OF EDUCATION

Being a student at Banneker was one of the most empowering and affirming experiences in my life. I had taken for granted my access to teachers and school administrators who are Black and Brown, that is, members of our community, and I realized after college just how lucky I was to see myself represented in positions of power and success. This taught me the true meaning of community development and has inspired the work that I do today. Currently, I am a tenure-track professor in the Department of Psychology, studying and teaching about the mental health effects of racism, oppression, and marginalization in the lives of racial and ethnic minority youth. Studying at Banneker certainly planted the seed for me to be where I am today. Careers in math and science were made to seem accessible and achievable for my peers and me. I am the first in my family to go to college, so the level of mentorship and the genuine investment the school and its staff made in me, shaped my confidence and commitment to serve my community. I truly feel like I hit the lottery by attending Banneker.

—L. Polanco, Class of 2002

The most challenging part of my job as a principal was dealing with the higher-ups. Problems and challenges were expected and came with the territory. However, administrator interference was draining. The Department of Education tried to influence what happened in our school. It was often about curriculum issues, but even what was on our walls or in our lesson plans sometimes became an issue.

When Dr. Young, the superintendent of District 13, was in charge, he consistently looked for ways to support our mission. He recommended hires, took part in our programs, and invited notable speakers to the school. He even joined our students on some trips. Dr. Young was a vital part of our school family, the wise community elder always there to offer advice and guidance.

He also shielded us from the higher-ups who wanted to interfere, and for this, he faced a lot of pushback on behalf of our school. One year, NYC Mayor Rudy Giuliani allegedly wanted to obtain the yearbook photos of all high school graduates so the police could use them to identify criminals. Dr. Young didn't allow this to happen. However, our relationship with the new power brokers changed when the governance changed, and he was no longer our superintendent. Banneker's relationship with the DOE became adversarial, and we had to fight to keep our school on the path we had envisioned. DOE administrators did not see our focus on promoting Black pride and excellence as a top priority. They wanted us to adopt a new curriculum, change teacher evaluation methods, and complete pointless, burdensome reports. We opposed many of the laissez-faire approaches to treating our children. We were tough on our kids because we understood the consequences of failure and all they were up against.

We sent teachers to the required professional development meetings. When they returned, we debriefed and decided if this new approach was right for our kids. We embraced some of the latest methods. Many, we didn't. We never attempted to publicly confront administrators when they came with mandates; we simply didn't implement them. If they tried to enforce something we didn't want, we pushed back forcefully with the might of the community behind us.

At one point, the DOE put in place a mandate that all high school students could be searched before entering the building. Unbeknownst to the school staff, police officers were sent to the school one morning and tried to use metal detectors to search our students. When parents found out, they were not happy. Our staff and parents didn't want our students to be treated as criminals, so we pushed back hard and convened an extensive meeting with higher-ups. The school auditorium was packed with parents, students, and community members. The parents made their opinions known, and department officials appeared shaken by the unified voices of our school family. They weren't expecting that level of solidarity and advocacy. We were not physically threatening, but our resolve was imposing. *Black love without concession was evident, and that's frightening for some folks.* This type of love was found in sit-ins and boycotts during the 1960s—strong, powerful, and resolute. The DOE reformed the measure, and moving forward, there would be no more unannounced searches.

Generally, the DOE found it best to leave us alone. At one of her staff meetings, a friend told me she had to warn the superintendent not to send a specific liaison to our school because it wouldn't go well. Intimidation tactics didn't work with Banneker, and we made that clear whenever needed. How could they tell us how to teach our children when we were successfully educating students, and they were eager to get into our building? *We were the all-Black school that was not to be messed with.*

Dealing with department administrators is a balancing act. I tell principals to tread lightly when confronted. Comply with mandates and deadlines whenever possible and push back only when necessary. Attend the meetings, cooperate when it benefits your students and teaching approach, and push back when it does not serve your goals. You must maintain your dignity, stand up for what you believe in, and when you must defy authority, ensure you have the backing of the school community. Eventually, if someone comes after you, you cannot fight alone. I don't know any effective principals who didn't have some higher-ups go after them at some point. The unions, some parents, and administrators will test your resolve. They have different agendas and may only care if their needs are addressed.

Always keep in mind the beautiful faces of our children. They are the ones who matter most—don't let others distract you with meaningless battles. Keep your focus.

As mentioned earlier, Dr. Young was very supportive, and I looked to him for guidance throughout my career. I remember fondly one piece of advice he gave me about handling stress as a school principal. (According to a recent Rand Corporation survey, principals are more than twice as likely as other working adults, even more likely than teachers, to report experiencing frequent job stress.)[19] Dr. Young shared that sometimes you need to get away from the stresses of your job, and when you need a break, you should take a short walk in the middle of the school day. I decided this was a great idea. The next stressful day, I left school around 11:30 that morning. I began walking around the community, greeting our neighbors as I passed by. I felt more relaxed and thought, *This is a great way to relieve stress.* I continued walking and entered a nearby park, where the flowers had started to bloom and the trees provided beautiful shade. I turned a corner and saw two Banneker students sitting on a park bench, cutting school, smoking marijuana, and just relaxing—so much for a stress-reducing stroll in the park. I guess they had the same idea I did. Needless to say, I broke that chill-fest up and escorted them back to school.

A huge point for me was that it was a smaller school. Most high schools I applied to were humongous, and that wasn't what I wanted for my experience. I cherish the idea of community, and Banneker definitely gave me that. I remember hanging out with my teachers after school or sometimes during, and having real conversations with them and fostering bonds. Another huge point about Banneker that stood out was the name of the school. You don't find many schools that are named after prominent African Americans, and that fostered the idea of Black power and wealth. Aside from my own love of history, Black history was taught and lived every day. I saw examples of Black men and women who fought against stereotypes placed on them. —B. Logo, Class of 2007

Within only a few short weeks, I quickly learned that Principal Rock carefully hand-selected each and every member of the staff within Benjamin Banneker Academy. I'd transferred in my sophomore year from a majority-white school in upstate New York and found myself in a historical training ground of a high school. Each and every woman stood as Queens who looked upon me as a daughter or sister they'd graciously lead. And I humbly followed suit, as every man greeted me with "Hey, sister"—the never-before felt gratitude of a daughter. Principal Daryl Rock stood ten feet tall as a watchman, kindred, or a king, inspiring and in full pursuit of opportunities for his future. We were his future. Truly an experience I could never forget. —S. Clark, Class of 2009

Principal's Office, Benjamin Banneker High School, Brooklyn, New York

March 2, 2001

Rock: Damn, Coach, that was a close first-round playoff win. What happened?

Coach: Kids were not ready. There was a lot going on. We were lucky to pull it out. We were down most of the game and just squeaked out a win at the buzzer, and we were playing one of the lowest seeds in the playoffs.

Rock: Our kids looked confused out there. That's the worst I have seen our guys play, Coach.

Coach: We scouted that team all wrong. We were playing a box-and-one against that one kid, but it wasn't working. They changed everything they did during the year. Smart coach over there.

Rock: They told me you went off in the locker room at halftime.

Coach: I had to, Rock. These playoff teams are tough.

Rock: Guys are playing hard, but it doesn't look like we are going to MSG this year. Maybe we need more experience.

Coach: Well, I don't know about that. Gary is back on the team.

11

BEAUTIFUL BLACK FACES

I felt seen at this school. I felt cared for. I felt family. I felt free, like I could do anything I wanted and be whoever I wanted to be. For the most part, whichever group we wanted to start at the school, the teachers and staff were behind us 1,000 percent and even stayed later at school to provide us the space to do so in their own classrooms. Classes felt like more than class. When I heard the experiences of other students from other schools, I knew that the staff at Banneker were going above and beyond to ensure our success and cultivate our growth in society.

—K. Alfonso, Class of 2010

It's hard to put into words how I feel about the students at our school. They were wonderful people who were fun to be around. Banneker felt like a school full of my own relatives. They were like sons, daughters, nieces, nephews, and cousins. We were all family. I felt pride when they showed me a good report card or book report. It was also rewarding when they brought me their failures, knowing that I wouldn't judge them harshly but would let them share their disappointments as we worked together to find solutions.

I tried to greet the students daily as they entered the building. Adolescence is a tough time, and it was impressive how our students managed this stressful period while still finding joy. You could hear laughter in the hallways and classrooms. These were happy children who felt safe in the building. I enjoyed walking the hallways after school and seeing young people interact with adults. Whether in the many teams, clubs, or informal conversations, admiration was shared by students and faculty alike. The kids could express themselves, but they also understood the boundaries. The teachers served as their mentors and important role models.

Some schools use community members and leaders as mentors, but I believe teachers make the best mentors. They have been properly vetted; you don't have to track them because they are in the building every day. Moreover, strong teachers know how to communicate and interact effectively with students. We supported the creation of teams and clubs so students would have accessible mentors ready to support them. We often assigned a staff member to mentor five students through the college application process. We intentionally created these groups, even though many of our student-teacher interactions were informal. You might be surprised how many academically talented students feel intimidated by the college application process. School staff must act as counselors and surrogates, especially when parental involvement is missing.

Seeing our children working diligently in the classroom brought me genuine joy and pride. I was delighted to witness their willingness to learn in classrooms, where mutual respect was evident. The classes all looked different: some had students sitting in a circle, some in groups, and others in clearly defined rows. Regardless of their setup, they all embodied Black achievement.

Banneker had outstanding students, but I don't want to give the impression that we didn't have any troublemakers. Some students could be confrontational. Sometimes, I had to escort an uncooperative student out of a classroom. We had defiant kids who refused to do assignments or participate in class, but not many. I worked at a specialized high school and faced more disciplinary problems than I ever did at Banneker. Even though I had high expectations for our students, I was pleasantly surprised by how much respect the staff and I received. I rarely raised my voice, yet the kids followed my directives.

On my way home late one evening, I saw three of our girls hanging out at a pizza shop a few blocks from the school. They were with three older gang members who were not students. I walked into the shop and said in a not-too-harsh tone, "Go home." Surprisingly, not only did the girls jump up and leave, but the gang members did, too.

Part of the reason for the compliance was my position of authority. The students also saw me as an older family member they didn't want to disappoint. I don't know why the gang members jumped up and left. Maybe they saw the command as one given out of genuine concern and familial care.

We had an overall graduation rate of 98 percent when I left Banneker. All the students with special needs also graduated that year. We tried not to isolate these students from their peers, and when they went to the Resource Room, they received help from some of the school's strongest teachers. We knew how to address a child's needs without stigmatizing or labeling them. The best special education teachers find ways to help their students understand that their disability does not define them. That label can strip away a student's dignity if they are made to feel less than their peers. I recommend that parents *avoid* testing their children for a learning disability if their school lacks an effective guidance and special education department.

I want to thank the students of Benjamin Banneker for helping me fulfill my life's calling in profound and beautiful ways. It was all so worthwhile—the struggles and the achievements. My lengthy career in education has been meaningful because of the success of many of these young people. When I walk the streets of Brooklyn now and run into former students, it warms my heart to see them smile as they remember their time at the school. I have come across my students in Georgia, Virginia, Chicago, and as far away as Barbados. Seeing me takes them back to the Banneker experience. They are reminded of a joyful, safe, and supportive place. Their insightful quotes throughout this book exemplify that. We were a family, living and embodying Black love. We created a special place that won't easily be forgotten.

Whenever I see former students, I am surprised by how much they have grown. They are adults now, many with children of their own. Their children are now *my children*, Ms. Murray's children, Dr. Young's children, Roger Green's children, George Leonard's children, Ms. Fischer's children, Coach Saunders' children, and Ms. Davidson's children. They are the children of our early Black educators. They belong to all of us, who share a collective responsibility for the success of future generations.

Principal's Office, Benjamin Banneker High School, Brooklyn, New York

March 6, 2001

Rock: Much better game, Coach. Kids played under more control. Did you guys really go to Restoration Plaza last night and order your players out of the party?

Coach: Yeah, Rock, they all wanted to go to Hakeem's birthday party.

Rock: I heard it was a nice party. No drama. Just our kids. No outsiders. Almost half the school.

Coach: At 10:00 p.m., we got all the players out of there. Just walked in and said, "Time to go."

Rock: Ten, Coach? The party had just started. Did you have the crew with you?

Coach: You know that.

Rock: Players didn't mind?

Coach: They minded, Rock, but we are trying to go to The Garden, and they needed rest.

Rock: Good thing you did because they played well. You made your daughter leave the party, too?

Coach: Nah. I thought about it, but she was having a good time, and there was no trouble. I didn't want to embarrass her in front of her friends. I picked her up later.

Rock: How many teachers do you think have their kids in our school?

Coach: A lot. Says something about the school, Rock.

Rock: Two more games to go. Let's go, Warriors.

12

THE CHARGE

Not only was I overprepared for my next step at Vanderbilt University academically, but I knew my history and who I was. When I stepped onto the campus, the culture shock didn't scare me. I was able to speak up about my experiences and my truth with confidence, even if I was the only *one* in my classes. I always speak of my time at Banneker with a smile on my face. Whether it was recalling the amazingness of nine-to-nines, learning to play spades in Fischer's room, the playful competition in Turner's English class, or editing the first magazine-style yearbook, I'm forever grateful for my time there and how it helped to shape the woman I am today.

—A. Richards, Class of 2004

I challenge all educators to find their purpose and pursue it with the same vigor and determination as the early Black teachers in segregated Southern schools. They never gave up because they knew the importance of their work. Teachers today have the same charge.

PRINCIPLES FOR PRINCIPALS

Throughout my more than forty years in education, I have embraced a core set of philosophies and ideas that have served me well while guiding tens of thousands of students. These principles were refined through a good deal of trial and error. I share some of them here in hopes of making the leadership journey easier for newer educators. Even experienced educators can benefit from these principles that worked effectively for us at Banneker Academy.

First, focus your time and energy on recruitment rather than training, since the right adults can truly transform your school. Don't waste time trying to change your staff's belief systems. If teachers are unwilling or unable to change, it's essential to develop an exit strategy for them. Do not let them stay in your school, as they will harm your students. When hiring teachers, value exemplary character over knowledge or certificates, as character is harder to change. When evaluating potential teachers, have them give mock lessons and always contact their previous school for feedback.

It's essential to greet students outside the building in the morning and ensure staff and security are present along their route home to demonstrate your concern for student safety. Visiting every teacher's classroom daily, even for just a few minutes, is beneficial. Provide ample support to strong teachers and offer solid after-school programs with the best instructors. Support teachers who introduce Black and other diverse cultures into the school. Promote cultural programs and activities both within and outside the school. Take the trips, whether local, national, or international. Make the additional effort; you'll see the transformation in your students.

Collaborate with students, parents, and staff to raise all necessary funds. The group effort will foster deeper connections and opportunities for cultivating respect, communal support, and building confidence in your students.

Give your teachers autonomy, but make sure they adhere to established standards while maintaining a firm approach. It's necessary to establish a visible presence in the community where your school is and welcome politicians, parents, and community leaders into the building. Choose partnerships that align with your school's agenda and mission. High school principals should focus on supporting ninth graders, ensuring they have strong teachers and the necessary credits to progress. That foundation is vital to students' success throughout the four-year journey. Once first-year students fall behind, it's difficult to catch up. Lead by example and demonstrate through your actions how you expect students to behave and be treated. Building mutual respect early in the education process is a quality worth developing. This will impact many aspects of student and adult life.

As principals, teaching a class and encouraging other administrators to do the same can be highly beneficial. It's important and helpful to experience firsthand what your teachers face in their classrooms every day.

Treat parents with the same warmth and kindness as you would treat your family, even in the face of confrontations with disgruntled parents. While maintaining respectful communication with your bosses, make it clear that you are committed to doing what's best for your students. Despite any challenges, always strive to maintain an upbeat demeanor and keep a smile on your face. Read the quotes from our graduates and consider whether this is the caliber of students you want to develop as future leaders. If so, return to work with renewed vigor and a fresh outlook. Our students need quality teachers and other adults to help them unleash the power they intrinsically have.

MESSAGE TO SCHOOL DISTRICTS

If school districts want to make a change, they need to go into colleges, especially Black colleges, and recruit young Black teachers with strong character who show promise. The certification rules for new teachers should be relaxed, and housing options should be available, particularly in expensive urban areas like New York City. School districts should involve the community in hiring school leaders, make it easier to dismiss underperforming teachers, and increase the recruitment budget threefold. They should also partner with high schools and colleges to develop effective training programs for future teachers. It's crucial for school districts to understand that mean-spirited teachers must not interact with students. I cannot emphasize this enough. The damage caused by an inappropriate, misguided teacher without students' best interests in mind can cause severe, lifelong trauma. I have seen this too often, and principals must not tolerate this destructive behavior.

Principal's Office, Benjamin Banneker High School, Brooklyn, New York

March 12, 2001

Rock: Well, Coach, another great game. One more win, and we go to MSG—the world's most famous arena. You gotta hand it to Gary. He really played well. He wasn't taking bad shots. Moved the ball and played under control. Looked like he bought into the system. That was a good team we played.

Coach: We wouldn't have won that game without Gary.

Rock: No, Coach, but look how well the other kids played.

Coach: I know—with poise.

Rock: Kareem and Gary kept the guys focused. Guards played strong. You guys did a good job bringing Gary into the mix. He didn't mess up the chemistry. Let's see how we do in the next game. How come the new kid showed up late?

Coach: Rock, believe it or not, he said he fell asleep, and his mom didn't wake him. Coach Williams had to go all the way to East New York to get him. When he got there, the kid was asleep. Drove him and his mom to the Bronx. They had no phone.

Rock: You guys all travel to the games on the train together, right?

Coach: We had to leave him. In the back of my mind, I think he was too nervous and didn't want to play.

Rock: Maybe so, Coach. It's a lot of pressure on these kids. Glad he got there because he played pretty good. Next game: Aviation High School. I saw them play. They are strong.

Coach: We will be fine.

13
CONCLUSION

Banneker was like a mecca of Black excellence. Most importantly, Banneker instilled in me that there is greatness in African American people. There was beauty in everything I saw, from natural hair and locs to language, Greek life, culture, experience, and enduring through pain. I long to be able to afford my own children a similar experience. Unfortunately, I think it could only come from Banneker.

—E. Turner, Class of 2003

On my last day at Banneker, I thanked all the teachers for giving me the chance to fulfill my childhood dream, which started on that first day of middle school. Banneker showed that our children can stay in our neighborhood and get a quality education. Black educators who believe in and see themselves in their students can help develop exceptional, high-achieving students.

Why hasn't this model been replicated throughout the city and state? That is the million-dollar question for those in charge. One might wonder: *Do school districts really want Black students to achieve and even excel, or is the status quo of underachievement more comfortable to accept and publicly lament over?*

When I left Banneker and worked as a superintendent, I asked an intern to look up all the high schools in New York State to find out which ones had done a great job of graduating Black students. She found a state document that disaggregated all the high schools and detailed their performance with Black students and graduation rates. She listed them in order for me. Banneker was the top school. She didn't know my connection to Banneker, and I didn't know where our school would rank.

"Do you know this school?" She asked.

"Yes, they were my family," I said.

"Wow! How did you do this?"

"The adults in the school were able to connect with Black children and inspire them."

As we talked, I reflected on the middle school I attended as a thirteen-year-old in that white neighborhood. I remembered the hatred and vitriol I faced and my determination to someday help create a safe space for Black children to learn in our community. Tears welled up in my eyes, just like they did that day in the auditorium so many years ago, but this time, they weren't tears of sadness caused by racial hatred. Instead, my tears were for a deep sense of achievement and contribution to the growth of African American students. I hoped the ancestors would be proud.

Being a child who moved a lot, coming to NYC was scary, but the first day I toured Banneker, it moved something in me. It was the first school that was clean, bright, and full of life, and the way they taught made me want to come to school every day. I learned during my time there about Blackness and the importance of community in such a way that it still impacts me today. I've never seen another school like it. I wish my child could experience the beauty of education the way that BBACD showed me. For everyone I knew from that school, life is different in a good way, which shaped us into better, positive, productive beings in society. —C. Doles, Class of 2001

Benjamin Banneker molded me into the person I am today. Benjamin Banneker was Howard University before I went to Howard University. A place where I can feel whole in my Blackness. A place where African culture was highlighted and celebrated. A place where I can indulge in activities not always allotted to young Black children in Brooklyn: the equestrian program, bowling, drama, Polytechnic University dual enrollment program for advanced mathematics students, architecture program, woodshop, media, African and modern dance, jazz band, and arts and crafts. We were exposed to so much. The teachers, principals, and staff members reflected who I wanted to be: Afrocentric. Powerful. Bold. Loving. Intelligent. Unique. Special. They truly cared. Benjamin Banneker, under the tutelage of Principal Daryl Rock, was a utopia in the middle of the hustle and bustle of Brooklyn. I am incredibly thankful and honored to have been a student during such a dynamic moment in educational history. I've always known my high school experience at Benjamin Banneker was beautiful, but the true magnitude of its magic did not hit me until this very moment. Much love and gratitude to Principal Daryl Rock for curating such a beautiful experience. Thank you! —D. Smith, Class of 2008

Thank you all!

Principal's Office, Benjamin Banneker High School, Brooklyn, New York

March 14, 2001

Rock: Kids did a pretty good job at the press conference today, Coach.

Coach: Yeah, Rock, I was more nervous than they were.

Rock: I remember they always have the press conference right before the finals at The Garden. How many kids can you bring to the conference?

Coach: Just two—brought three, though.

Rock: Can you believe we are going to play in MSG?

Coach: I had confidence all year, and the kids really believed they could win the championship.

Rock: Glad you brought your crew to the conference.

Coach: They played just as important a role as I did. I couldn't leave them out.

Rock: A lot of coaches don't allow other voices, but you encouraged it. Showed a lot of class.

Coach: They are my guys. That's what the great coach Ray Haskins taught me. Respect your assistant coaches.

Rock: That was a terrific semi-final win, beating Aviation High School 61 to 48. Saw Gary had 20, and Kareem had 13.

Coach: Yeah, Rock, I hope they can do the same against Thurgood Marshall in the finals.

Rock: Well, we're going to Madison Square Garden? Can't wait.

Coach: Rock, you gonna sit on the bench?

Rock: No, I will be in our section. Want to be with our family. This accomplishment is important because people need to see that a strong academic school can have a great basketball team. Our kids are not geeks or nerds.

Coach: Nope. They're smart, and they can play ball!

Rock: Regular kids from the community can excel in the classroom and on the basketball court if the right adults are around them. I am really proud of this team and the girls' team, who made it to the quarterfinals. Great job, Coach. Thurgood Marshall is good, but your guys will compete and play hard. It doesn't matter who wins; your guys got us here. Quite an accomplishment. Got a lot of calls for tickets. I had to give tickets to all the folks who played a role in the formation of the school. Assemblyman Roger Green and Superintendent Dr. Young will be front and center.

HONORING THE WARRIOR TEACHERS

Exemplary teachers, staff members, and community leaders made Benjamin Banneker Academy the high school success story it became. This book was written out of my deep appreciation, sincere love, and lasting respect for this incredible tribe, committed to educating and supporting Black children in the best possible ways. I am forever indebted to their brilliance and ingenuity.

I had the privilege of knowing and working with so many exceptional individuals in our school community. Ms. Al Shafi, my guardian, provided unwavering support throughout each school day and helped me survive my principalship. Mr. Aristilde, a master teacher, left a lasting impression with his dedicated approach to teaching. Mr. Blayne's impact was profound, as he provided invaluable support and guidance to our students. Mr. Bumachar had strong skills in teaching mathematics. Mr. Caicedo made an incredible difference, offering much-needed support to struggling students. Ms. Charles, whom I affectionately referred to as my *work daughter,* was not only a great person, but also an outstanding teacher. It was rewarding to witness Ms. Collica's growth into a remarkable Banneker educator during my tenure.

Ms. Coleman's history classes were informative, engaging, and delivered with style. Mr. Conway, our professional developer, shared invaluable knowledge with us all. Ms. Cook-Person created an inviting and safe classroom environment that helped our students thrive. Mr. Corbie, our young dean, was skilled at disciplining with compassion. That is a skill every teacher should nurture and develop throughout their career. Ms. Council was a dedicated counselor who filled me with pride because of her diligence, compassion, and accomplishments—my real-life goddaughter.

Mr. Crawford's mentorship impacted many of our young men, and he was instrumental in advancing the school's community development mission.

As a steady leader, Ms. Crooks guided us through each day with remarkable composure. Mr. Daughtry was affectionately known as *Mr. Computer Guy* for his expertise in the field. Ms. David, the star of paraprofessionals, was a dedicated mentor to our students. Mr. Derrick created a unique mural for us, and his creativity was evident in his innovative teaching methods. Ms. Dupree excelled as both a student and a teacher, leaving a lasting impact in both roles. Mr. Egashira's classes were always filled with respect and conviction, making him a student favorite. Mr. Ellis exemplified the qualities of a true gentleman, scholar, and all-around class act. Mr. Fernandez used baseball to teach important life lessons. Mr. Fielder's skills as a media expert and filmmaker greatly influenced our students. Ms. Fisher was a brilliant maestro in the classroom, and her students were stronger because of it.

Ms. Ford had a beautiful talent for teaching the art of writing, as well as, an appreciation for the written word. Ms. Garraway organized a transformative trip to Europe for our students. Ms. Green did remarkable work with students with special needs. She was outstanding. Mr. Green (no relation), our athletic director, helped many coaches succeed on the court. Mr. Grissett's *Work Hard, Play Hard* approach made him a great teacher, father, and gentleman. Ms. Haywood's extraordinary journey from a powerful educator to an exemplary principal was inspiring to see. Mr. Henry's talent for teaching pre-calculus was impressive, and his depth of mathematical knowledge was truly commendable. Watching Mr. Higgins grow from a high school student to a strong, confident leader has been very rewarding. Ms. Iverson's students contributed significantly to the inspiring cultural artwork adorning the many walls of Banneker. Ms. Jamison, our resident filmmaker, provided our kids with a vital platform to tell their stories using film. I admire Ms. Jeffries, who taught exceptionally well and was like a daughter to me.

Mr. Johnson, a Banneker alumnus, became a stellar educator. Ms. Johnson (no relation) was our dance teacher who taught us all the power of movement. Mr. Laprede gave many of our students great hope through his caring nature. Mr. Leonard was the G.O.A.T. of educators, leaving an unparalleled legacy. Ms. Majida's noble leadership and spirited nature left a lasting impact on all of us. She replaced me and took the school to new heights. Ms. Mathews was a great teacher who became an even greater leader. Mr. McBeth's role as counselor and community advocate was commendable. Mr. Middleton, one of our talented paraprofessionals, was hardworking and committed as he took on challenging tasks with our students. Mr. Miller's expertise in teaching English was instrumental in preparing our seniors for life after high school. Mr. A. Muhammad was a great teacher who became an exemplary principal.

Mr. Y. Muhammad (no relation) had a skillful journey from being an excellent teacher to a brilliant principal. His role as a dedicated father and student mentor showcased his potential for outstanding accomplishments.

Mr. Mulgrave's skills as a baseball coach and a teacher had a profound impact on students. Ms. Murray, *my work wife*, was the heart and soul of the school. Mr. Murray's (no relation) mentorship was vital in guiding and keeping our young men grounded. Ms. Pacheco's contribution as an educator was simply remarkable. Mr. Pierce's role as a young educator left an indelible mark on so many of those he taught. Mr. Plummer's transition from our Assistant Coach to Head Coach, leading his team to a city championship, was incredible to see. Mr. Pryce's role as my dependable and loyal colleague in the fight to educate our children was invaluable. Mr. Ravenell, our personal *Duke Ellington,* played a pivotal role in teaching our kids to appreciate the history of our music.

Ms. Renee was a skilled math teacher who later became an outstanding school leader. Ms. Richmond's scholarly expertise, historical knowledge, and adroitness in teaching made her one of the very best. Ms. Robinson and Mr. Underwood, our Principal Interns, both went on to become talented, effective leaders. Our Queen Mother, Ms. Samuels, opened the African diaspora for all of us, leaving a life-long impression. Ms. T. Samuels was a superb, no-nonsense English teacher. Mr. Sanford had a remarkable ability to connect well with parents and students, which helped create a positive school environment. His son, David, everyone's favorite, who recently passed away, was a student at Banneker who had a unique style, was culturally conscious, and brilliant in the classroom—a devastating loss for our entire family. Mr. Sanni had terrific success working with challenging students. Mr. Saunders, our stellar basketball coach, led us to the championship game at Madison Square Garden twice! Mr. Senior excelled in teaching basketball and motivational skills, and our kids were the beneficiaries.

Mr. Shabaka's role as *Mr. African Street Festival* and *Man of the People* showcased his commitment to the community. Ms.

Sinckler, *my goddaughter*, was a remarkable history teacher and someone who made me immensely proud. Mr. Smalls could connect with young people whom others found difficult to reach, showcasing his compassionate nature. Ms. Solomon, our guidance counselor extraordinaire, showcased our students' creativity through legendary fashion shows. Mr. Stanley's way of managing the cafeteria was spot on. Ms. Stevens was an outstanding special education teacher who became a strong leader. Ms. Summers, our art teacher, had terrific style and talents. Ms. Tate, affectionately known as *Ms. Kinship Association*, and her husband were dedicated volunteers and my favorite parents. Ms. C. Thomas, a talented administrator, is destined to be a great principal one day. Ms. A. Thomas (no relation) had impeccable organizational skills that kept us all on time, present, and accounted for.

Mr. Thompson is a young warrior educator who has risen to great heights. Mr. Titley taught biology with such class. Mr. Tuggle was my No. 1 son, and I'm very proud of the man he has become. Ms. Toppin was our French teacher, who set the standard for excellence. Mr. Turner taught English like no one else, connecting with students on another level, and Mr. Ueda held the after-school programs together. I must say, Ms. Urena *eres la mejor profesîra de Espanol.* Additionally, Ms. Venable personified class with her beautiful voice and ensured the office ran smoothly. Ms. Wali was a very caring teacher, while Ms. Williams was our computer technology pro and a good friend. Ms. B. Williams (no relation) was our physical education teacher who inspired young minds in critical ways. Mr. Williams (no relation) was a great teacher, coach, friend, and community activist. Ms. Woods was the quintessential guidance counselor who set our kids on excellent career paths. Ms. Wright-Lewis was our gifted author and Poet-in-Residence, and I loved her two kids.

Then there were those exceptional Banneker educators who passed away, leaving their indelible impressions on our hearts and minds. Mr. Abney played a crucial role in introducing many of our students to HBCUs. Mr. Barclift was a community advocate, cultural sage, eminent artist, and beloved family member. Mr. Bishop was a wonderful mentor, and the kids loved him. Ms. Davidson was *Ms. Banneker* and co-principal with me. She made it all happen. Mr. T. Fisher changed our thinking about technology. He had such a brilliant mind and a wonderful spirit. Ms. Kinard was the teacher with the longest tenure at Banneker and touched many young lives. Ms. Nolen was a beautiful spirit who uplifted us all. Mr. Rogers was our *Mr. Everything*, and Mr. Saahki was our first IT guy, dedicated to our staff and students. Mr. Smith, *my brother*, made chemistry understandable and interesting. Ms. E. Tate was our classy librarian who gave so much to the school. They are all deeply missed and fondly remembered for their many contributions. If I have inadvertently left anyone off this Warrior list, please blame the passage of time and not ill will. This is all done in love!

Principal's Office, Benjamin Banneker High School, Brooklyn, New York

March 18, 2001, 11:00 p.m.

Rock: You did it, Coach! 60 to 56. City Champs! What a game! Gary played a fantastic game, even though they gave the MVP to Kareem.

Coach: It could have gone to Gary, but Kareem was just as deserving. He played real hard. He also made those two free throws with seventeen seconds left!

Rock: Yeah, all the kids played with poise. I'm really proud of what you and the other coaches did, shaping our players.

Coach: You see how many students are in the building this time of night, Rock? More than half the school.

Rock: On their own, they all just gravitated to the school from MSG. I know it's a little crazy at this time of night, but I guess, with all the excitement, they felt like they wanted to celebrate at home with the family.

ACKNOWLEDGMENTS

This book documents my ten-year relationship with the stellar students and staff of Benjamin Banneker Academy for Community Development in Brooklyn, New York. The school had a rich history before I arrived, and it has had a storied history since I've been gone. Before I arrived, Frank Spradley was the principal who left to accept a superintendent position. Mr. Spradley created the school's Afrocentric, family-oriented atmosphere. He started the Kinship Association and supported co-principal Ms. Davidson and me when we began our respective tenures. He is a revered educator and activist in Central Brooklyn, and I am eternally thankful for his expansive vision and dedicated service to the community. There is a story to be told about the school's founding, its early years, and its present life. I hope someone will take that on someday.

I want to sincerely thank several individuals who played a key role in Banneker Academy's success. I must acknowledge Roger Green, the local politician, who, around thirty-five years ago, envisioned building a high school in the Fort Greene section of Brooklyn and had the dogged determination to see it through to completion. He worked with community members, advocates, and leaders, including then-Mayor David Dinkins, to garner the necessary support for this major undertaking. Together, this group accomplished something unprecedented at the time. The community took the initiative to create a school, not the Department of Education or government officials, and they did this in 1993. I hope Assemblyman Green has the chance to read the many heartfelt messages from students about their years at Banneker, and that he takes pride in knowing his dream of a school where students learn the importance of giving back is thriving. Without Roger Green's innovative thinking and relentless efforts, Banneker would not exist.

I must acknowledge Superintendent Dr. Lester Young for continually reminding us to focus on the "main thing"—educating and preparing young minds without excuses, because failure was never an option. The staff and I knew he was in our corner whenever we faced challenges, and there were certainly many struggles and obstacles along the way. He was the first administrator I worked with who understood the importance of students knowing their history and celebrating their culture. He and his deputy, Ms. Douglas, supported us during our many complex exchanges with disgruntled teachers and the teachers' union. Dr. Young is an educator's educator, and I thank him for his mentorship, stewardship, and fellowship during my tenure as principal at Banneker Academy and the years since then.

For those who don't know, George Leonard is the G.O.A.T. of all science teachers. He has a way of relating to Black children that is firm yet endearing. Kids love him and see him as their protector. Many young people would not have been successful today had they not crossed paths with George Leonard years ago. He was our school dean who kept order in the most caring, disciplined manner. Students respected him deeply, and he was the driving force in creating order. He set the tone for the school and the parents. He was at Banneker for my first three years before forming an outstanding school in Brooklyn, where he received the city's highest annual report card rating. His reputation is known throughout the city. His educational acumen and powerful character would be the answer to the Black educational problem in America if his traits could only be replicated.

Ms. Pearl Davidson shared school leadership with me for three years when I arrived at Banneker. She was the most dedicated educator I knew. Her tireless resolve helped Banneker and its students thrive. Ms. Davidson had a strong, confident, and nurturing way with people. She was an expert in the art of teaching and was highly respected by her peers. She reminded me of those strong, determined early Black teachers. Her life and approach provided wonderful examples for many teachers who loved and learned so much from her. She passed away in the fall of 2014, but her spirit as an educator still resonates strongly with many. We all miss her.

Ms. Valerie Murray, *my work wife*, was a key figure in the Banneker success story. She tolerated me, offered advice, and was the person I turned to during crises. We shared laughter, disagreements, and tears. She was often my right and left hand. Her loving, motherly nature allowed her to mentor many children and adults. I remember on September 11, 2001, she united staff and students with her strong yet compassionate approach, making us feel secure amidst the chaos and horror of that day. Our school faced the burning WTC towers across the East River. Several of our students had parents working in the towers, creating many anxious moments as we watched the buildings collapse. Ms. Murray was exceptional that day, and her leadership helped us navigate through the tough situation. Schools don't achieve high graduation rates without a dedicated guidance department. Ms. Murray led the department and made sure her staff built genuine connections with students. She was with me from day one until I left Banneker ten years later. I am forever grateful for her support, loyalty, and guidance.

A heartfelt thank you to Ms. Crooks, the Assistant Principal, who kept us all afloat with her steady hand and endearing personality.

A heartfelt thank you to all the students who sent in the remarkable quotes. They made this story authentic. Sorry, I couldn't use all of them.

Thank you to Coach Saunders, Coach Williams, and Coach Plummer for the many hours they spent on the phone with me reminiscing about our championship season. Also, thank you to the basketball players, boys and girls, for bringing so much excitement and pride to our school community.

I must thank my editors, Amanda Bauch, Marcia Fingal, Brandy Patton, and Serena Springle, for approaching this work with devotion and deep respect for the subject. I am forever grateful.

A special thank you to my parents, Dr. Edith Rock and Dr. Alfonso Rock, for providing safe places for my sisters, JoAnn, Lynette, and Allyson, and me to be educated, and for insisting that we maintain strong ties to our community and history even when we were in predominantly white environments.

Finally, I extend my profound gratitude to those early Black educators of the segregated South. Despite facing harsh conditions and racial hostility, they successfully guided Black students toward achievement. Let us pay tribute to their countless contributions by actively preserving and advancing their legacy.

The End

ENDNOTES

1   https://www.p12.nysed.gov/irs/cohort/2010/200809rpt-school-raceeth.pdf.

2   Adair, *A Desegregation: The Illusion of Black Progress.* Lanham, Md: University Press of America 1984, p 122.

3   Quinn, David M., and Tara-Marie Desruisseaux. (2022). Replicating and Extending Effects of "Achievement Gap" Discourse. (EdWorkingPaper: 22-628). Retrieved from Annenberg Institute at Brown University: https://doi.org/10.26300/2pky-ch12.

4   https://www.chalkbeat.org/newyork/2023/10/4/23904023/nyc-test-scores-state-exam-math-reading-disparities/.

5   The Silent Epidemic. *Statistics and Facts About High School Dropout Rates.* Retrieved from http://www.silentepidemic.org/resources/policymakers.htm.

6   The Hamilton Project…Ten Economic Facts about Crime and Incarceration in the United States By: Melissa S. Kearney, Ben Harris, Elisa Jácome, Lucie Parker 2014.

7   Swisher RR, Dennison CR. Educational Pathways and Change in Crime Between Adolescence and Early Adulthood. J Res Crime Delinq. 2016 Nov;53(6):840-871. doi: 10.1177/0022427816645380. Epub 2016 May 4. PMID: 28348441; PMCID: PMC5365088.

8   Franklin, John Hope and Alfred A. Moss, Jr. From Slavery to Freedom: A History of African Americans, 7th ed. New York: Knopf, 1994, page 230, 264-268.

9   https://www.archives.gov/education/lessons/freedmen#toc-related-primary-sources.

10   Woodson, Carter G., The Rural Negro. Washington, D.C.: Association for the Study of Negro Life and History, 1930, 184-185.

11   Walker, Vanessa, Their Highest Potential, Chapel Hill: North Carolina Press, 1996, page 3.

12   Sowell, Thomas. Patterns of Black Excellence: Public Interest 43 (1976): 26-58.

13   Walker, Vanessa, Their Highest Potential, Chapel Hill: North Carolina Press, 1996, page 3.

14   Malcolm X Quotes. (n.d.). BrainyQuote.com. Retrieved October 2, 2024, from BrainyQuote.com Web site: https://www.brainyquote.com/quotes/malcolm_x_379120.

15   Helen Keller. https://deniselescano.com/helen-keller/.

16   (Editorial. Newsweek, 18 July 1994, p 54.)

17   Resnick, L.B. Making America Smarter. Education Week Century Series. (1999, June 16). p 18, 38–40.

18   Liu, J., Penner, E., & Wenjing, G. (2023). Troublemakers? The role of frequent teacher referrals in expanding racial disciplinary disproportionalities. *Educational Researcher*. Prepublished June 15, 2023. https://www.doi.org/10.3102/0013189X231179649.

19   ascd (2022, October 1). *The difficult job of school leaders*. www.Ascd.org. Retrieved May 28, 2024, from https://www.ascd.org/el/articles/the-difficult-job-of-schools-leaders.